EZRA TAFT BENSON

MARY ELLEN EDMUNDS

VAUGHN J. FEATHERSTONE

MARION D. HANKS

ARDETH G. KAPP

SPENCER W. KIMBALL

ANN N. MADSEN

Prayer

TRUMAN G. MADSEN

NEAL A. MAXWELL

BRUCE R. McCONKIE

ROBERT L. MILLET

H. BURKE PETERSON

CAROLYN J. RASMUS

MARION G. ROMNEY

N. ELDON TANNER

DESERET
BOOK

SALT LAKE CITY, UTAH

Library of Congress Cataloging-in-Publication Data

Prayer.— Rev. ed.
   p. cm.
  Includes index.
  ISBN 1-59038-530-6 (hardbound : alk. paper)
   1. Prayer—Church of Jesus Christ of Latter-day Saints. 2. Mormon
Church—Doctrines. 3. Church of Jesus Christ of Latter-day
Saints—Doctrines. I. Deseret Book Company.
  BV210.3.P73 2005
  248.3'2—dc22   2005018692

Printed in the United States of America
Worzalla Printing Company, Stevens Point, WI

10 9 8 7 6 5 4 3 2 1

Contents

Why the Lord Ordained Prayer
  Elder Bruce R. McConkie 1

Why We Should Pray
  President Marion G. Romney 15

What Should We Pray For?
  Elder Neal A. Maxwell 21

Prayer, the Soul's Sincere Desire
  Mary Ellen Edmunds 32

The Intimate Touch of Prayer
  Truman G. Madsen 57

Improving Communication with
Our Heavenly Father
  President Ezra Taft Benson 75

Preparation for Prayer
  Elder Marion D. Hanks 82

Pray with All Energy of Heart
  Ann N. Madsen 93

Family Prayer
  President Spencer W. Kimball 111

CONTENTS

Teaching Our Children to Pray
  Elder Vaughn J. Featherstone 117

Adversity and Prayer
  Bishop H. Burke Peterson 126

Pray Always and Be Believing
  Carolyn J. Rasmus 132

Communion with the Infinite
  Robert L. Millet 144

The Power of Prayer
  President N. Eldon Tanner 158

Keeping in Touch
  Ardeth Greene Kapp 169

Index 181

Why the Lord Ordained Prayer

ELDER BRUCE R. McCONKIE

O N THE WEST wall of the Council of the Twelve room in the Salt Lake Temple hangs a picture of the Lord Jesus as he prays in Gethsemane to his Father. In agony beyond compare, suffering both body and spirit, to an extent incomprehensible to man—the coming torture of the cross paling into insignificance—our Lord is here pleading with his Father for strength to work out the infinite and eternal atonement.

Of all the prayers ever uttered, in time or in eternity—by gods, angels, or mortal men—this one stands supreme, above and apart, preeminent over all others.

In this garden called Gethsemane, outside Jerusalem's wall, the greatest member of Adam's race, the One whose every thought and word were perfect, pled with his Father to come off triumphant in the most torturous ordeal ever imposed on man or God.

There, amid the olive trees—in the spirit of pure worship and perfect prayer—Mary's Son struggled under the most crushing burden ever borne by mortal man.

There, in the quiet of the Judean night, while Peter, James, and John slept, God's own Son—with prayer on his lips—took upon himself the sins of all men on conditions of repentance.

Upon his Suffering Servant, the great Elohim, there and then, placed the weight of all the sins of all men of all ages who believe in Christ and seek his face. And the Son, who bore the image of the Father, pled with his divine Progenitor for power to fulfill the chief purpose for which he had come to earth.

This was the hour when all eternity hung in the balance. So great was the sin-created agony—laid on him who knew no sin—that he sweat great drops of blood from every pore, and "would," within himself, that he "might not drink the bitter cup." (D&C 19:18.) From creation's dawn to this supreme hour, and from this atoning night through all the endless ages of eternity, there neither had been nor would be again such a struggle as this.

"The Lord Omnipotent who reigneth, who was, and is from all eternity to all eternity," who had "come down from heaven among the children of men" (Mosiah 3:5); the Creator, Upholder, and Preserver of all things from the beginning, who had made clay his tabernacle; the one person born into the world who had God as his father; the very Son of God himself—in a way beyond mortal comprehension—did then and there work out the infinite and eternal atonement whereby all men are raised in immortality, while those who believe and obey come forth also to an inheritance of eternal life. God the Redeemer ransomed men from the temporal and spiritual death brought upon them by Adam's fall.

And it was at this hour that he, who then bought us with his own blood, offered the most pleading and poignant personal prayer ever to fall from mortal lips. God the Son prayed to God the

Father, that the will of the one might be swallowed up in the will of the other, and that he might fulfill the promise made by him when he was chosen to be the Redeemer: "Father, thy will be done, and the glory be thine forever." (Moses 4:2.)

True, as an obedient son whose sole desire was to do the will of the Father who sent him, our Lord prayed always and often during his mortal probation. By natural inheritance, because God was his father, Jesus was endowed with greater powers of intellect and spiritual insight than anyone else has ever possessed. But in spite of his superlative natural powers and endowments—or, shall we not rather say, because of them (for truly the more spiritually perfected and intellectually gifted a person is, the more he recognizes his place in the infinite scheme of things and knows thereby his need for help and guidance from Him who truly is infinite)—and so by virtue of his superlative powers and endowments, Jesus above all men felt the need for constant communion with the Source of all power, all intelligence, and all goodness.

When the time came to choose the twelve special witnesses who should bear record of him and his law unto the ends of the earth, and who should sit with him on twelve thrones judging the whole house of Israel, how did he make the choice? The inspired account says, "He went out into a mountain to pray, and continued all night in prayer to God." Having thus come to know the mind and will of him whose offspring he was, "when it was day, . . . he chose twelve, whom also he named apostles." (Luke 6:12–13.)

When the hour of his arrest and passion were at hand; when there remained one more great truth to be impressed on the Twelve—that if they were to succeed in the assigned work and merit eternal reward with him and his Father they must be one even as he and the Father were one—at this hour of supreme import, he taught the truth involved as part of his great intercessory prayer, fragments of which are preserved for us in John 17.

When he, after his resurrection—note it well: after his resurrection, he was still praying to the Father!—when he, glorified and perfected, sought to give the Nephites the most transcendent spiritual experience they were able to bear, he did it, not in a sermon, but in a prayer. "The things which he prayed cannot be written," the record says, but those who heard bore this testimony:

"The eye hath never seen, neither hath the ear heard, before, so great and marvelous things as we saw and heard Jesus speak unto the Father;

"And no tongue can speak, neither can there be written by any man, neither can the hearts of men conceive so great and marvelous things as we both saw and heard Jesus speak; and no one can conceive of the joy which filled our souls at the time we heard him pray for us unto the Father." (3 Nephi 17:15–17.)

But here in Gethsemane, as a pattern for all suffering, burdened, agonizing men, he poured out his soul to his Father with pleadings never equaled. What petitions he made, what expressions of doctrine he uttered, what words of glory and adoration he then spoke we do not know. Perhaps like his coming prayer among the Nephites the words could not be written, but could be understood only by the power of the Spirit. We do know that on three separate occasions in his prayer he said in substance and thought content: "O my Father, if it be possible, let this cup pass from me: nevertheless not as I will, but as thou wilt." (Matthew 26:39.)

Here in Gethsemane, as he said to his Father, "not my will, but thine, be done," the inspired record says, "There appeared an angel unto him from heaven, strengthening him.

"And being in an agony he prayed more earnestly: and his

sweat was as it were great drops of blood falling down to the ground." (Luke 22:42–44.)

Now here is a marvelous thing. Note it well. The Son of God "prayed more earnestly"! He who did all things well, whose every word was right, whose every emphasis was proper; he to whom the Father gave his Spirit without measure; he who was the only perfect being ever to walk the dusty paths of planet earth—the Son of God "prayed more earnestly," teaching us, his brethren, that all prayers, his included, are not alike, and that a greater need calls forth more earnest and faith-filled pleadings before the throne of him to whom the prayers of the saints are a sweet savor.

In this setting, then, seeking to learn and live the law of prayer so that we, like him, can go where he and his Father are, let us summarize what is truly involved in the glorious privilege of approaching the throne of grace. Let us learn how to do so boldly and efficaciously, not in word only but in spirit and in power, so that we may pull down upon ourselves, even as he did upon himself, the very powers of heaven. Perhaps the following ten items will enable us to crystallize our thinking and will guide us in perfecting our own personal prayers.

1. What prayer is. Once we dwelt in our Father's presence, saw his face, and knew his will. We spoke to him, heard his voice, and received counsel and direction from him. Such was our status as spirit children in the pre-earth life. We then walked by sight.

Now we are far removed from the divine presence; we no longer see his face and hear his voice as we then did. We now walk by faith. But we need his counsel and direction as much as or more than we needed it when we mingled with all the seraphic hosts of heaven before the world was. In his infinite wisdom, knowing our needs, a gracious Father has provided prayer as the means of continuing to communicate with him. As I have written elsewhere:

"To pray is to speak with God, either vocally or by forming the thoughts involved in the mind. Prayers may properly include expressions of praise, thanksgiving, and adoration; they are the solemn occasions during which the children of God petition their Eternal Father for those things, both temporal and spiritual, which they feel are needed to sustain them in all the varied tests of this mortal probation. Prayers are occasions of confession—occasions when in humility and contrition, having broken hearts and contrite spirits, the saints confess their sins to Deity and implore him to grant his cleansing forgiveness." (*Mormon Doctrine,* 2d ed. [Salt Lake City: Bookcraft, 1966], 581.)

2. **Why we pray.** There are three basic and fundamental reasons why we pray:

   a. *We are commanded to do so.* Prayer is not something of relative insignificance that we may choose to do if the fancy strikes us. Rather, it is an eternal decree of Deity. "Thou shalt repent and call upon God in the name of the Son forevermore," was his word in the first dispensation. "And Adam and Eve, his wife, ceased not to call upon God." (Moses 5:8, 16.) In our day we are instructed: "Ask, and ye shall receive; knock, and it shall be opened unto you." (D&C 4:7.) Home teachers are appointed in the Church to "visit the house of each member, and exhort them to pray vocally and in secret." (D&C 20:47.) And speaking by way of commandment to his latter-day people, the Lord says, "He that observeth not his prayers before the Lord in the season thereof, let him be had in remembrance before the judge of my people." (D&C 68:33.)

   b. *Temporal and spiritual blessings follow proper prayer.* As all the revelations show, the portals of heaven swing wide open to those who pray in faith; the Lord rains down righteousness upon them; they are preserved in perilous circumstances; the earth yields her fruits to them; and the joys of the gospel dwell in their hearts.

c. *Prayer is essential to salvation.* No accountable person ever has or ever will gain celestial rest unless he learns to communicate with the Master of that realm. And, "how knoweth a man the master whom he has not served, and who is a stranger unto him, and is far from the thoughts and intents of his heart?" (Mosiah 5:13.)

3. Pray to the Father. We are commanded to pray to the Father (Elohim) in the name of the Son (Jehovah). The revelations are perfectly clear on this. "Ye must always pray unto the Father in my name," the Lord Jesus said to the Nephites. (3 Nephi 18:19.) And yet there is an amazing mass of false doctrine and false practice in the churches of Christendom and occasionally even among the true Saints.

There are those who pray to so-called saints and plead with them to intercede with Christ on their behalf. The official prayer books of the various sects have some prayers addressed to the Father, others to the Son, and others to the Holy Spirit, and it is the exception rather than the rule in some quarters when prayers are offered in the name of Christ. There are those who feel they gain some special relationship with our Lord by addressing petitions directly to him.

It is true that when we pray to the Father, the answer comes from the Son, because "there is . . . one mediator between God and men, the man Christ Jesus." (1 Timothy 2:5.) Joseph Smith, for instance, asked the Father, in the name of the Son, for answers to questions, and the answering voice was not that of the Father but of the Son, because Christ is our advocate, our intercessor, the God (under the Father) who rules and regulates this earth.

And it is true that sometimes in his answers, Christ assumes the prerogative of speaking by divine investiture of authority as though he were the Father; that is, he speaks in the first person and uses the name of the Father because the Father has placed his own name on the Son.

It is also true that we and all the prophets can with propriety shout praises to the Lord Jehovah (Christ). We can properly sing unto his holy name, as in the cry "Hallelujah," which means "praise Jah," or "praise Jehovah." But what we must have perfectly clear is that we *always* pray to the Father, not the Son, and we *always* pray in the name of the Son.

4. Ask for temporal and spiritual blessings. We are entitled and expected to pray for all things properly needed, whether temporal or spiritual. We do not have the right of unlimited petition; our requests must be based on righteousness. "Ye ask, and receive not, because ye ask amiss, that ye may consume it upon your lusts." (James 4:3.)

Amulek speaks of crops and herds, of fields and flocks, as well as of mercy and salvation, when he lists those things for which we should pray. (See Alma 34:17–29.) The Lord's Prayer speaks of "our daily bread" (see Matthew 6:11), and James urges us to ask for wisdom (see James 1:5), which in principle means we should seek all of the attributes of godliness. Our revelation says, "Ye are commanded in all things to ask of God." (D&C 46:7.) Nephi says, "Ye must not perform any thing unto the Lord save in the first place ye shall pray unto the Father in the name of Christ, that he will consecrate thy performance unto thee, that thy performance may be for the welfare of thy soul." (2 Nephi 32:9.) And the Lord's promise to all the faithful is: "If thou shalt ask, thou shalt receive revelation upon revelation, knowledge upon knowledge, that thou mayest know the mysteries and peaceable things—that which bringeth joy, that which bringeth life eternal." (D&C 42:61.)

It is clear that we should pray for all that in wisdom and righteousness we should have. Certainly we should seek for a testimony, for revelations, for all of the gifts of the Spirit, including the fulfillment of the promise in Doctrine and Covenants 93:1 of seeing the face of the Lord. But above all our other petitions, we should plead for the companionship of the Holy Ghost in this life and for eternal life in the world to come. When the Nephite Twelve "did pray for that which they most desired," the Book of Mormon account records, "they desired that the Holy Ghost should be given unto them." (3 Nephi 19:9.) The greatest gift a man can receive in this life is the gift of the Holy Ghost, even as the greatest gift he can gain in eternity is eternal life.

5. Pray for others. Our prayers are neither selfish nor self-centered. We seek the spiritual well-being of all men. Some of our prayers are for the benefit and blessing of the Saints alone; others are for the enlightenment and benefit of all our Father's children. "I pray not for the world," Jesus said in his great intercessory prayer, "but for them which thou hast given me." (John 17:9.) But he also commanded, "Love your enemies, bless them that curse you, do good to them that hate you, and pray for them which despitefully use you, and persecute you." (Matthew 5:44.)

And so, just as Christ "is the Saviour of all men, specially of those that believe" (1 Timothy 4:10), so we pray for all men, but especially for ourselves, our families, the Saints in general, and those who seek to believe and know the truth. Of especial concern to us are the sick who belong to the household of faith and those who are investigating the restored gospel. "Pray one for another, that ye may be healed," James says, with reference to church members, for "the effectual fervent prayer of a righteous man availeth much."

(James 5:16.) And as to those who attend our meetings and who seek to learn the truth, the Lord Jesus says, "Ye shall pray for them unto the Father, in my name," in the hope that they will repent and be baptized. (3 Nephi 18:23. See also verse 30.)

6. **When and where to pray.** "Pray always." (2 Nephi 32:9.) So it is written—meaning: Pray regularly, consistently, day in and day out; and also, live with the spirit of prayer always in your heart, so that your thoughts, words, and acts are always such as will please Him who is Eternal. Amulek speaks of praying "both morning, mid-day, and evening," and says we should pour out our souls to the Lord in our closets, in our secret places, and in the wilderness. (Alma 34:17–29.) Jesus commanded us to hold both personal and family prayer: "Watch and pray always," he said; and also, "Pray in your families unto the Father, always in my name, that your wives and your children may be blessed." (3 Nephi 18:15, 21.)

The practice of the Church in our day is to have family prayer twice daily, plus our daily personal prayers, plus a blessing on our food at mealtimes (except in those public or other circumstances where it would be ostentatious or inappropriate to do so), plus proper prayers in our meetings.

7. **How to pray.** Always address the Father; give thanks for your blessings; petition him for just and proper needs; and do it in the name of Jesus Christ.

As occasion and circumstances require and permit, confess your sins; counsel with the Lord relative to your personal problems; praise him for his goodness and grace; and utter such expressions of worship and doctrine as will bring you to a state of oneness with him whom you worship.

Two much-overlooked, underworked, and greatly needed guidelines for approved prayer are these:

a. *Pray earnestly, sincerely, with real intent, and with all the energy and strength of your soul.* Mere words do not suffice. Vain repetitions are not enough. Literary excellence is of little worth. Indeed, true eloquence is not in excellence of language (although this should be sought for), but in the feeling that accompanies the words, however poorly they are chosen or phrased. Mormon said, "Pray unto the Father with all the energy of heart." (Moroni 7:48.) Also, it is "counted evil unto a man, if he shall pray and not with real intent of heart; yea, and it profiteth him nothing, for God receiveth none such." (Moroni 7:9.)

b. *Pray by the power of the Holy Ghost.* This is the supreme and ultimate achievement in prayer. The promise is, "The Spirit shall be given unto you by the prayer of faith" (D&C 42:14), "and if ye are purified and cleansed from all sin, ye shall ask whatsoever you will in the name of Jesus and it shall be done." (D&C 50:29.) Of the coming millennial era, when prayers shall be perfected, the scripture says, "And in that day whatsoever any man shall ask, it shall be given unto him." (D&C 101:27.)

8. **Use both agency and prayer.** It is not, never has been, and never will be the design and purpose of the Lord—however much we seek him in prayer—to answer all our problems and concerns without struggle and effort on our part. This mortality is a probationary estate. In it we have our agency. We are being tested to see how we will respond in various situations; how we will decide issues; what course we will pursue while we are here walking, not by sight, but by faith. Hence, we are to solve our own problems and then to counsel with the Lord in prayer and receive a spiritual confirmation that our decisions are correct.

As he set forth in his work of translating the Book of Mormon, Joseph Smith did not simply ask the Lord what the characters on the plates meant; rather, he was required to study the matter out in his mind, make a decision of his own, and then ask the Lord if his conclusions were correct. (See D&C 8 and 9.) So it is with us in all that we are called upon to do. Prayer and works go together. If and when we have done all we can, then in consultation with the Lord, through mighty and effectual prayer, we have power to come up with the right conclusions.

9. **Follow the formalities of prayer.** These (though many) are simple and easy and contribute to the spirit of worship that attends sincere and effectual prayers. Our Father is glorified and exalted; he is an omnipotent being. We are as the dust of the earth in comparison, and yet we are his children with access, through prayer, to his presence. Any act of obeisance that gets us in the proper frame of mind when we pray is all to the good.

We seek the guidance of the Holy Spirit in our prayers. We ponder the solemnities of eternity in our hearts. We approach Deity in the spirit of awe, reverence, and worship. We speak in hushed and solemn tones. We listen for his answer. We are at our best in prayer. We are in the divine presence.

Almost by instinct, therefore, we do such things as bow our heads and close our eyes, fold our arms, or kneel, or fall on our faces. We use the sacred language of prayer (that of the King James Version of the Bible—*thee, thou, thine,* not *you* and *your.*) And we say *amen* when others pray, thus making their utterances ours, their prayers our prayers.

10. **Live as you pray.** There is an old saying to this effect. "If you can't pray about a thing, don't do it," which is intended to tie our prayers and acts together. And true it is that our deeds, in large measure, are children of our prayers. Having prayed, we act; our proper petitions have the effect of charting a righteous course of conduct for us. The boy who prays earnestly and devoutly and in

faith that he may go on a mission, will then prepare himself for his mission. The young people who pray always, in faith, to marry in the temple, and then act accordingly, are never satisfied with worldly marriage. So intertwined are prayer and works that having recited the law of prayer in detail, Amulek then concludes:

"After ye have done all these things, if ye turn away the needy, and the naked, and visit not the sick and afflicted, and impart of your substance, if ye have, to those who stand in need—I say unto you, if ye do not any of these things, behold, your prayer is vain, and availeth you nothing, and ye are as hypocrites who do deny the faith." (Alma 34:28.)

We have now spoken, briefly and in imperfect fashion, of prayer and some of the great and eternal principles that attend it. There remains now but one thing more—to testify that these doctrines are sound and that prayer is a living reality which leads to eternal life.

Prayer may be gibberish and nonsense to the carnal mind, but to the saints of God it is the avenue of communication with the Unseen. To the unbelieving and rebellious it may seem as an act of senseless piety born of mental instability, but to those who have tasted its fruits it becomes an anchor to the soul through all the storms of life.

Prayer is of God—not the vain repetitions of the heathen, not the rhetoric of the prayer books, not the insincere lispings of lustful men, but that prayer which is born of knowledge, which is nurtured by faith in Christ, which is offered in spirit and in truth.

Prayer opens the door to peace in this life and eternal life in the world to come. Prayer is essential to salvation. Unless and until we make it a living part of us so that we speak to our Father and have his voice answer, by the power of his Spirit, we are yet in our sins.

> *O, thou by whom we come to God,*
> *The Life, the Truth, the Way!*

The path of prayer thyself hast trod;
Lord, teach us how to pray.
> *("Prayer is the Soul's Sincere Desire,"* Hymns of The
> Church of Jesus Christ of Latter-day Saints *[Salt Lake*
> *City: The Church of Jesus Christ of Latter-day Saints, 1985],*
> *no. 145)*

Of all these things I testify, and pray to the Father in the name of the Son that all of the Latter-day Saints, as well as all those in the world who will join with them, may—through prayer and that righteous living which results therefrom—gain peace and joy here and an eternal fulness hereafter.

Why We
Should Pray

PRESIDENT MARION G. ROMNEY

RECENTLY SOMEONE asked, Why should we pray? We should pray because prayer is indispensable to the accomplishment of the real purpose of our lives. We are children of God. As such, we have the potentiality to rise to his perfection. The Savior himself inspired us with this aspiration when he said, "I would that ye should be perfect even as I, or your Father who is in heaven is perfect." (3 Nephi 12:48.)

No one shall ever reach such perfection unless he is guided to it by Him who is perfect. And guidance from Him is to be had only through prayer. In our upward climb, this mortal experience through which we are now passing is a necessary step. To obtain perfection, we had to leave our pre-earth home and come to earth. During the transfer, a veil was drawn over our spiritual eyes, and the memory of our pre-earth experiences was suspended. In the Garden of Eden, God endowed us with moral agency and, as it were, left us here on our own between the forces of good and evil to be proved—to see if, walking by faith, we would rise to our high potentiality by doing "all things whatsoever the Lord [our] God shall command [us]." (Abraham 3:25.)

The first instruction the Lord gave Adam and Eve, following their expulsion from Eden, was to pray. (See Moses 5:5.)

During his mortal ministry, Jesus taught "that men ought always to pray." (Luke 18:1.)

To the Nephite multitude he said, "Ye must always pray unto the Father in my name." (3 Nephi 18:19.)

In this last dispensation, two years before the Church was organized, the Lord, in a revelation to the Prophet Joseph Smith, said: "Pray always, that you may come off conqueror; yea, that you may conquer Satan, and that you may escape the hands of the servants of Satan that do uphold his work." (D&C 10:5.)

Later he added, "What I say unto one I say unto all; pray always lest that wicked one have power in you, and remove you out of your place." (D&C 93:49.)

The experience of the brother of Jared dramatizes the seriousness of disobeying the commandment to pray. From the tower of Babel the Lord led the Jaredite colony to the seashore where they "dwelt in tents . . . for the space of four years.

"And . . . at the end of four years . . . the Lord came again unto the brother of Jared, and stood in a cloud and talked with him. And for the space of three hours did the Lord talk with the brother of Jared, and chastened him because he remembered not to call upon the name of the Lord.

"And the brother of Jared repented of the evil which he had done, and did call upon the name of the Lord for his brethren who were with him. And the Lord said unto him: I will forgive thee and thy brethren of their sins; but thou shalt not sin any more, for ye shall remember that my Spirit will not always strive with man;

wherefore, if ye will sin until ye are fully ripe ye shall be cut off from the presence of the Lord." (Ether 2:13–15.)

The sin of which he was guilty was neglecting his prayers.

The foregoing scriptures give adequate reasons why we should pray. There seems to be no limitation as to when, where, and what we should pray about.

"In every thing by prayer and supplication with thanksgiving let your requests be made known unto God." (Philippians 4:6.)

"Yea, cry unto him for mercy; for he is mighty to save.

"Cry unto him when ye are in your fields, yea, over all your flocks.

"Cry unto him in your houses, yea, over all your household, both morning, mid-day, and evening.

"Yea, cry unto him against the power of your enemies.

"Yea, cry unto him against the devil, who is an enemy to all righteousness.

"Cry unto him over the crops of your fields, that ye may prosper in them.

"But this is not all; ye must pour out your souls in your closets, and your secret places, and in your wilderness.

"Yea, and when you do not cry unto the Lord, let your hearts be full, drawn out in prayer unto him continually for your welfare, and also for the welfare of those who are around you." (Alma 34:18, 20–24, 26–27.)

"Pray in your families unto the Father, always in my name," said the Savior, "that your wives and your children may be blessed." (3 Nephi 18:21.)

"Pray vocally as well as in thy heart; yea, before the world as well as in secret, in public as well as in private." (D&C 19:28.)

"Call upon the Lord, that his kingdom may go forth upon the earth, that the inhabitants thereof may receive it, and be prepared for the days to come, in the which the Son of Man shall come down in heaven, clothed in the brightness of his glory, to meet the kingdom of God which is set up on the earth.

"Wherefore, may the kingdom of God go forth, that the kingdom of heaven may come, that thou, O God, mayest be glorified in heaven so on earth, that thine enemies may be subdued; for thine is the honor, power and glory, forever and ever. Amen." (D&C 65:5–6.)

Prayer is the key that unlocks the door to communion with Deity. "Behold," said the Lord, "I stand at the door, and knock: if any man hear my voice, and open the door, I will come in to him, and will sup with him, and he with me." (Revelation 3:20.)

A similar promise, as Jesus gave it to the Nephites, is: "Whatsoever ye shall ask the Father in my name, *which is right,* believing that ye shall receive, behold it shall be given unto you." (3 Nephi 18:20; emphasis added.)

To us of this last dispensation, the promise is thus stated: "Whatsoever ye ask the Father in my name it shall be given unto you, *that is expedient for you."* (D&C 88:64; emphasis added.)

The sacred records are replete with proof that such promises are fulfilled.

Prayer brought forgiveness of sins to Enos. (See Enos 1:4–5.) The prayers of Alma Senior sent an angel to bring his son Alma to repentance. (See Mosiah 27:14.) Prayer brought the Father and the Son to visit the Prophet Joseph Smith. (See Joseph Smith—History 1:14–17.) Prayer brought the seagulls from the lake to help save the crops of the pioneers.

Not every prayer brings a spectacular response, but every sincere and earnest prayer is heard and responded to by the Spirit of the Lord. The manner in which answers to prayer most frequently come was indicated by the Lord when he said to Oliver Cowdery:

"Verily, verily, I say unto you, if you desire a further witness, cast your mind upon the night that you cried unto me in your heart, that you might know concerning the truth of these things.

"Did I not speak peace to your mind concerning the matter? What greater witness can you have than from God?" (D&C 6:22–23.)

To all of us in this last dispensation, the Lord has given this promise: "If you will ask of me you shall receive; if you will knock it shall be opened unto you." In seven different revelations, the Lord repeats this promise—D&C 6:5; 11:5; 12:5; 14:5; 49:26; 66:9; 75:27.

In the Doctrine and Covenants he further says:

"I say unto you, my friends, I leave these sayings with you to ponder in your hearts, with this commandment which I give unto you, that ye shall call upon me while I am near—

"Draw near unto me and I will draw near unto you; seek me diligently and ye shall find me; ask, and ye shall receive; knock, and it shall be opened unto you.

"Whatsoever ye ask the Father in my name it shall be given unto you, that is expedient for you." (D&C 88:62–64.)

To the truth of these promises, I bear my own testimony; I know they are true.

I know that prayers are answered. Like Nephi and Enos of old, I was born of "just" and "goodly" parents. Early in my childhood I was trained to kneel at my bedside morning and evening each day and thank my Heavenly Father for his blessings and petition him for his continued guidance and protection. This procedure has remained with me through the years.

In answer to prayer as a child, I found my lost toys; as a youth, in answer to prayer, I was led to find the cows in a thicket. I am familiar with the feeling spoken of by the Lord when, to Oliver

Cowdery, he said: "Did I not speak peace to your mind concerning the matter?" (D&C 6:23.) He further said: "Behold, I say unto you, that you must study it out in your mind; then you must ask me if it be right, and if it is right I will cause that your bosom shall burn within you; therefore, you shall feel that it is right. But if it be not right you shall have no such feelings, but you shall have a stupor of thought." (D&C 9:8–9.)

I know what Enos meant when he said that "the voice of the Lord came into my mind again." (Enos 1:10.) By this means I have received in sentences answers to my prayers.

I have witnessed the fulfillment of the Lord's promise that "whoso shall ask . . . in my name in faith, they shall cast out devils; they shall heal the sick; they shall cause the blind to receive their sight, and the deaf to hear, and the dumb to speak, and the lame to walk." (D&C 35:9.)

I have put Moroni's promise to the test, and in answer to my prayers I have received a divine witness that the Book of Mormon is true. I further know that by praying "with a sincere heart, with real intent, having faith in Christ," one may "by the power of the Holy Ghost" receive a knowledge of "the truth of all things." (See Moroni 10:4–5.)

I bear my personal solemn testimony that prayer is the key that unlocks the door to communion with Deity.

What Should We Pray For?

ELDER NEAL A. MAXWELL

THERE ARE SO MANY instructive examples of prayer in the scriptures! The very variety of examples requires us to sort out the strategic things with regard to the purposes of our petitions and the content of our prayers.

In the Book of Mormon we read that the Savior directed, "Whatsoever ye shall ask the Father in my name, *which is right,* believing that ye shall receive, behold it shall be given unto you." (3 Nephi 18:20; emphasis added.)

This is one of the most significant and distinctive insights given to us in all of the scriptures. Even though we may ask in faith for something, unless it is right for us, God reserves the decision-making power to himself. A perfect, loving, and omniscient Father would do just that. Thus, in addition to having faith, we need to ask for that which is right. This same tonal truth appears in modern revelations. The Lord told the Prophet Joseph Smith, "Whatsoever ye ask the Father in my name it shall be given unto you, that is *expedient* for you." (D&C 88:64; emphasis added.)

Clearly, the Lord reserves the right to determine that which is best for us, lest we ask for something in our spiritual naïveté that would not conform to the will of God. Nephi, the prophet, understood the importance of precision and propriety in prayer. He knew from happy experience that God would give liberally to him if he, Nephi, prayed in such a way that he "ask not amiss." (2 Nephi 4:35.)

Thus we see the importance of what a modern prophet has told us. President Joseph F. Smith asserted that spiritual growth includes "the education of our desires." (*Gospel Doctrine,* [Salt Lake City: Deseret Book, 1939], 297.) Our task is to come to that point in our progress where our very desires are right in the sight of God. When we arrive at that point, we will have the "mind of Christ." (1 Corinthians 2:16.) From those with the "mind of Christ" will come perfect prayers.

Continuing to speak of strategic things, we must have the Spirit with us, so that the Holy Ghost can prompt us to pray for that which is right. Nephi advised us that the Spirit "teacheth a man to pray." (2 Nephi 32:8.) There is, therefore, a definite connection between our righteousness and our capacity to draw upon the Spirit so that we will ask for what we should ask for. The Lord told Joseph Smith in 1831, "And if ye are purified and cleansed from all sin, ye shall ask whatsoever you will in the name of Jesus and it shall be done. But know this, it shall be *given* you what you shall ask." (D&C 50:29–30; emphasis added.)

Obviously this purposeful praying reflects a high order of spirituality. For those of us less far along in the path of prayer, these insights at first might seem quite discouraging, because while the promises are valid, we feel so distant from that point when "it shall be given you what you shall ask." Even so, we need to understand the significance of these scriptures if we are to move very far along the path of prayer by learning to pray for correct things as well as developing our faith. Only then will our prayers deserve to be characterized as "counsel[ing] with the Lord in all [our] doings." (Alma 37:37.)

One might ask, "Why is it necessary that the Holy Ghost prompt us even in our prayers?" One reason is that only with the help of the Holy Ghost can we be lifted outside the narrow little theater of our own experience, outside our selfish concerns, and outside the confines of our tiny conceptual cells. It was Jacob who reminded us, and in such beautiful language, that the Spirit (which teaches us to pray) also "speaketh of things as they really are, and of things as they really will be." (Jacob 4:13.) The Spirit "searcheth . . . the deep things of God" (1 Corinthians 2:10), and superficial prayer will not produce such probings.

God sees things as they really are and as they will become. We don't! In order to tap that precious perspective during our prayers, we must rely upon the promptings of the Holy Ghost. With access to that kind of knowledge, we would then pray for what we and others should have—*really* have. With the Spirit prompting us, we will not ask "amiss."

With access to the Spirit, our circles of concern will expand. The mighty prayer of Enos began with understandable self-concern, moved outward to family, then to his enemies, and then outward to future generations.

Lest one become prematurely discouraged because of the less lofty patterns in his own prayers, remember that we can grow in experience in prayer as in all things. The Prophet Joseph Smith on one occasion said, "A person may profit by noticing the first intimation of the spirit of revelation; for instance, when you feel pure intelligence flowing into you, it may give you sudden strokes of ideas, so that by noticing it, . . . you may grow into the principle of revelation, until you become perfect in Christ Jesus." (*Teachings of the Prophet Joseph Smith,* comp. Joseph Fielding Smith [Salt Lake City: Deseret Book, 1976], 151.) When our prayers are inspired, we actually learn from our very petitions, just as President Marion G. Romney has observed that when he speaks under inspiration, he learns from what he says.

To be able to tap divine perspective, with regard to the content of our petitions, thus becomes exceedingly important. Otherwise we might pray for a job that wouldn't be right for us. We might ask "amiss" in terms of removing a challenge before us, when what we need is help in order to cope with that challenge. There are ever so many ways in which we must come to be guided even in the content of our prayers. It is not enough to kneel, important as that is, or to have faith, as essential as that is. We must come to bend our will to the will of God, so that in our prayers we really commune with him and ask for those things which are right.

The Lord has told us with regard to truth, and presumably this would include truths about ourselves and our own circumstances— the very things about which we pray so often—that "truth is knowledge of things as they are, and as they were, and as they are to come." (D&C 93:24.) This connection of the past with present circumstances and with the future provides a convergence of truth that can give us precious perspective about ourselves and our circumstances. Such perspective would undoubtedly alter the objects of our sometimes petty petitions or narrow and naive requests to our Heavenly Father. Hopefully, we will never forget that "all things . . . past, present, and future . . . are continually before the Lord." (D&C 130:7.)

Meanwhile, it should not cause dismay in ourselves or others that there are gradations of spiritual perceptivity. People can witness the same phenomenon and understand it in varying degrees. In one of his marvelous prayers, Jesus prayed with such earnestness and power that "then came there a voice from heaven," referring to the glorification of the name of God. When the voice of heaven came, the scriptures tell us, "the people therefore, that stood by, and heard it, said that it thundered: others said, An angel spake to him. Jesus answered and said, This voice came not because of me, but for your sakes." (John 12:28–30.)

Perhaps there were some who heard nothing at all; some who heard the sound but thought it to be thunder; some who recognized it as a voice but did not understand the words; some who thought it was the voice of an angel; and some who knew it was the voice of God.

Having said these strategic things, let us now look at what we learn in the scriptures about proper prayers, so far as the content of these petitions is concerned.

The obvious tactical truths are that we can appropriately pray for many things: for forgiveness, for strength, for direction over our daily affairs, for leaders, for family, and for mankind. We also ought to have as the purpose of some prayers sheer adoration. But having generalized, let us examine the record for appropriate models.

Moses, when Israel had sinned, was asked by his people to "pray unto the Lord, that he take away the serpents from us." Under these circumstances "Moses prayed for the people." (Numbers 21:7.) It is significant that Moses prayed for the people in spite of the fact that many of them were unworthy of the practical blessing they sought; they failed to take advantage of the instrument (the brass serpent upon the pole) that was provided so that if they were bitten by the fiery serpents they had only to look in order to be healed. Moses prayed anyway.

In the Book of Mormon we find a striking insight into a somewhat parallel circumstance in which Mormon prayed for the people but acknowledged that it was a prayer "without faith," because of the exceeding wickedness of the people. However, Mormon kept praying. (Mormon 3:12.)

It is also appropriate for us to pray for leaders and for helpers. Jesus did this in praying for his disciples. Significantly he said, "I pray not that thou shouldest take them out of the world, but that thou shouldest keep them from the evil." (John 17:15.) The Lord did not ask for an exemption for his followers. Praying for others that they shall overcome indicates that all temptation and trials are not to be removed from our pathway. Prayers are not to be bulldozers that automatically clear the way of all roadblocks.

In the Book of Mormon, Jesus instructed his followers to pray for their wives and children. (3 Nephi 18:21.) We should do so—and by name—so that our family members hear themselves being prayed over.

Obviously, we should pray when leaders are being selected. In Samuel's selection of Saul, under the inspiration of heaven, we read of the systematic search for a new king. It was work—real work—as family after family came before Samuel. Upon inquiring of the Lord, the Lord indicated that the man to be crowned "hath hid himself." The people ran and fetched Saul, "and when he stood among the people, he was higher than any of the people from his shoulders and upward." (1 Samuel 10:22–23.) Virtually every weekend, General Authorities of the Church pray, for instance, as men are chosen to preside over stakes. It is an appropriate object of prayer; indeed, it is a necessity.

We know that the Prophet Joseph Smith prayed for forgiveness of his sins. He said on one occasion, "I betook myself to prayer and supplication to Almighty God for forgiveness of all my sins and follies, and also for a manifestation to me, that I might know of my state and standing before him." (Joseph Smith—History 1:29.) Surely each of us has many occasions when such petitions are necessary.

Daniel was esteemed. The scriptures tell us that "an excellent spirit was in him." (Daniel 6:3.) He apparently prayed on his knees at least three times a day, facing Jerusalem and giving thanks before his God. Daniel's prayers were prayers of thanksgiving, were sincere, and were regularized before he was placed in the den of lions. It is significant that King Darius, who had reluctantly placed Daniel in that den of lions, fasted for Daniel's safety and slept not. (See Daniel 6:18.) Regularity in praying does not mean that our prayers must be ritualized or become routine.

The object of some prayers is more obvious, though still not inappropriate, than others. Some objects are apt to be subtle and soul-stretching. For instance, one of the ways of testing ourselves is to ask ourselves how often we have actually followed the injunction from the Savior in which he said that we should pray for those who despitefully use us and persecute us. (Matthew 5:44.) How often have we specifically prayed for those who use, abuse, manipulate, and exploit us?

How often do we praise the Lord "with a prayer of praise and thanksgiving"? (D&C 136:28.) As noted earlier, some prayers ought to be prayers of sheer adoration. Adoration, absent of any petition, even occasionally would be a better mix than prayers that are perpetual petitions and relentless requests, minus adoration and appreciation.

Close examination of the Lord's Prayer (using the models given us in the New Testament and in the Book of Mormon) indicates the need for reverent salutation as we open the prayer; our expressed desire that the work and the will of God be accomplished; a request for our daily bread (not for an annuity or pension); a petition for reciprocal forgiveness (it would be wrong to pray for forgiveness unless we have a forgiving spirit ourselves); a desire to avoid temptation or to be delivered from evil; an indication of submission in which we acknowledge that the kingdom is God's and the glory is his.

On our own small scale we can, as Jesus did, pray that certain "cups" will pass from us. But we must also do as he did by saying, "Nevertheless not as I will, but as thou wilt." (Matthew 26:39.)

We can pray as Jesus did in his great high priestly prayer (John 17) in which he actually reviews his stewardship with a loving Father in heaven; he also prayed for his disciples, and for unity.

How often have we reviewed our stewardship in like manner, especially vocally? How appropriate that Jesus reviewed his stewardship just before the betrayal.

We can and should pray for effectiveness in our ministry so we will be able to speak God's word with effectiveness, whether as a Primary teacher or a missionary or whatever. The saints assembled after Jesus' ascension did so when they said, "Grant unto thy servants, that with all boldness they may speak thy word." Following this prayer "they were all filled with the Holy Ghost, and they spake the word of God with boldness." Significantly, when there was such communion and selflessness in prayer, "the multitude of them that believed were *of one heart* and of one soul." (Acts 4:29, 31–32; emphasis added.)

Paul urged us to "let [our] requests be known unto God" through "prayer and supplication with thanksgiving." (Philippians 4:6.) In the Book of Mormon, we are instructed to pray over our fields and over our flocks. And elsewhere in the Book of Mormon we are told to "counsel with the Lord in all [our] doings." (Alma 37:37.) God will think nothing trivial if it bears upon our salvation.

God never holds us in contempt. He smiles upon us, but never laughs at the childishness of our prayers, though we have an obligation to grow in the effectiveness of them.

Can we pray for inappropriate things? Of course we can. We can pray for wickedness *with* happiness; for status *and* humility. The Lord said that Martin Harris was not to trouble him further. (D&C 5:26–29.) There is a difference between pressing the Lord for something that is not right and importuning for something that is right. The test is the rightness of the request, not the span of time over which it is made. Protracted petitions (even when right) may be required, since persistence is sometimes necessary for us to grow.

We need to pray for confirmation of decisions we are about to make, noting that we are first to study it out in our minds. (D&C 9:8.) Some of us in our laziness attempt to use God as a research assistant.

What then might be said of the typical blocks, the common blocks, that get in our way when we struggle over what to pray for? First, there is a lack of realization on our part that we can actually be guided in terms of what we should pray for. We tend to *pour out* petitions without letting inspiration *pour in*. God can truly prompt us in our prayers to ask for that which is right, to not ask amiss. God can educate our desires.

We also sometimes fail to study things out in our mind before praying so that we do not fully frame our questions and petitions. Our petitions are often skimpy on the "whereas" and move too quickly to the "be it resolved" portion of prayer. Further, we sometimes deflect the promptings that come when we petition; these may be faint beginnings of our apprenticeship in prayer and in revelation.

We may sometimes inappropriately pray, in effect, to be taken out of the world rather than praying that we will be kept from evil and prevail.

We too often pray in generalities rather than specifics. A vague prayer is hardly a prayer at all.

We may be too embarrassed to bring before the Lord specific weaknesses we have, yet he knows of them anyway. We thus prevent ourselves from gathering and gaining the strength we might need to overcome them. Admitting aloud (though in private) our weaknesses and stating our promises is sometimes better than just thinking of them. Dealing with our specific weaknesses is far better than simply praying that we will be more righteous.

Fatigue tends to produce prayers that are hasty generalities. This suggests that to pray only just before retirement at the end of a taxing day is to adversely affect the content of our prayers.

Our unwillingness to deal boldly with our own problems tends to produce prayers in which the objects of the petitions are couched again in generalities.

Other chapters elsewhere in this book speak of other dimensions of prayer, but presumably, as with Enos, we could, if needed and prepared, engage "in mighty prayer" over many hours. (Enos 1:4.) Meanwhile, most of us should improve the quality of our briefer prayers. That would be a beginning. And in the beginning men began "to call upon the name of the Lord." (Genesis 4:26.) Without proper purpose we sometimes pray just so we can be seen or heard praying. Verily, we have our reward when people thus see or hear us pray. Surely we should expect no further reward from such vain prayer. The Savior referred to those who pray in this manner as hypocrites. (Matthew 6:5–8.) Vain repetition also obstructs, perhaps more than repetition *per se,* but we must beware well-worn phrases which denote laziness rather than freshness.

Finally, if we need to consult someone concerning the content of our prayers, we would do well to consult our conscience. By consulting our conscience, the obvious would assert itself, and the inappropriate content in prayer could disappear. We may pray and plead for someone to understand us, when (under the doctrine of Matthew 18:15) it is up to us to take the initiative in seeking out that person to end the impasse. Conscience can call us to account for such tactical matters.

There is a real risk that praying, therefore, for wrong things (or things which at least are not right) will immobilize us or leave us on a lower performance plateau, so that we never scale the heights to which real prayer could take us.

We are given an ultimate and stunning promise that takes us back to the opening paragraphs of this chapter. The Lord promises us, "He that asketh in the Spirit asketh *according to the will of God; wherefore it is done even as he asketh*." (D&C 46:30; emphasis added.) What power! What proximity!

It is out of the depths of true prayer that an individual rises to real heights. When Jesus "fell on his face" (Matthew 26:39), in prayer he drew close to the throne of his loving Father, and he thus drew strength to complete his divine mission "according to the will of God."

Prayer, the Soul's Sincere Desire

MARY ELLEN EDMUNDS

I LOST MY SCRIPTURES on February 7, 1991. Sometimes when you tell people you have lost something—for example, you might say, "I lost my scriptures," or "I lost my keys," or "I lost my testimony"—they say, "Well, where did you put it?" So in this case, people said to me, "Where did you put your scriptures?" And I said, "If I knew that, they wouldn't be lost!" The last place I remembered seeing them was in a zipper bag in Salt Lake City. I had gone to a meeting and had my hands full of things, so I laid my scriptures on the top of the car. I thought maybe I had left them there, so every time I drove to Salt Lake, I drove the same way because maybe they had bounced off and were in a ditch or something. I didn't want them to be desecrated or damaged.

I didn't realize I would miss them so much. I remember thinking earlier in my life that if I lost my scriptures I could always get some more. I hoped I would never lose my missionary journals or other things that I couldn't replace. As a little kid I would sit in sacrament meeting and hear really *old* people—the kind that can hardly make it up to the front—bear their testimonies. They would say, "I just love the scriptures." And I'd think, "You big liar. You don't really. You're just saying that because you're old and you're about to die and you figure you'd better say that so you can go to heaven." I thought that because I didn't yet love them. I didn't yet know enough about what was in the scriptures.

There used to be a joke—I don't think it applies to us anymore—that if all the Latter-day Saints took their copies of the Book of Mormon off their shelves and blew the dust off at the same time, there'd be an eclipse of the sun. I love the fact that now you see more and more of us bringing our scriptures with us to meetings. We cherish them. We love them. We read in them. I'm awed and amazed and thrilled at how many scriptures young people can quickly turn to and how they have made them a part of their lives.

I did miss my scriptures. I missed them a lot. Of course I prayed to find them. Two months went by and all of a sudden the still small voice came into my mind (it calls me Edmunds). It said, "Edmunds, your scriptures are gone. Go to the scripture store and get some new ones. It's almost time for general conference and you have to take scriptures with you to conference." So I went to the scripture store and bought a Bible and a triple combination. I paid for them and took them to conference, and I tried to be close to them. But they weren't user-friendly—I couldn't just turn to things, and I hadn't written my name in them because they didn't feel like mine. But I took them to conference and I tried to bond with them. I would hold them up and show them as the General Authorities came in. "Oh," I'd think, "that's Elder So-and-so. And oh, there are the sisters over there!"

A few days after conference, a little over two months after I had lost my scriptures, I decided to pray one more time. It was almost as if I was giving Heavenly Father one more chance to help me find them. I thought, "If they don't come back after one more earnest prayer, then I'll write my name in these new ones and get on with my life." I knelt down and talked to the Lord about them. It was as if I was proposing to play "Hot and Cold." I would wander around and he would say, "Cold . . . cold . . ." and then, "Warm . . . warm . . . warmer . . . warmer . . . ," and of course I would come upon my scriptures.

I did say to him that I didn't want to be annoying, but I really would love to find my scriptures. They really meant a lot to me—all the things I had written in the margins and the little bus tickets and all of the other treasures I had stored in there. I even loved the way they smelled after being in so many moldy climates. But I also said there would be no hard feelings if I couldn't have them back. I had hoped all along that maybe some nonmember had found them and was reading them, and that there would be a fabulous story about this person reading them and wanting to know more and wanting to be baptized!

The next morning I arrived at the Missionary Training Center too early to get in the door that was right by my office, so I went around to the lobby area. I thought, "Well, as long as I'm here I can pick up my mail." There are little slots to put our mail in, and if we receive something that is too big for the slot, a little green slip of paper is placed in the slot letting us know about the large item. The item is then placed in a holder on the top of the mailboxes. I pulled my things out of my mail slot that morning, and I found a little green slip. It said, "Sister Edmunds, an item for you that would not fit in your mailbox has been placed above the mailboxes. The item is your scriptures." I still have the actual little piece of green paper.

I immediately looked up. They weren't in a holder. They were just sitting up there on the top of the mailboxes. I could almost smell them already—that little moldy smell—and I think I almost fainted. I reached up and grabbed them and hurried down the hall into my office. I shut the door, locked it, knelt down, and just wept. That the Lord would look out on all his billions of children and find this one little whiny one who wants her scriptures back and respond so sweetly and bring them back to her—the wonder of it! To be able to talk to him about anything—and to realize that many, many times miracles happen, even little miracles.

"Try Praying"

I love titles. I notice titles. Several years ago I noticed an article in the newspaper because the title intrigued me: "Try Praying This Year." I knew I wanted to read this article. It started out this way: "Looking for a happier new year? A recent university study examining what contributes to a greater sense of well being found a curious factor. Certain types of prayer. They found that frequent prayer heightens happiness, general life satisfaction and religious satisfaction."

What a great study! I can imagine people in white lab coats with 12,000 rats—6,000 of them pray and 6,000 don't pray, and these fellows are there taking notes. "Oh, they're frowning over here—they seem happier on this side." They could have saved a lot of money, a lot of rats, and a lot of time if they had just consulted the scriptures. For example, Doctrine and Covenants 19:38 records a message Joseph Smith received for Martin Harris in which the Lord taught, "Pray always, and I will pour out my Spirit upon you, and great shall be your blessing." In 2 Nephi 32:8, toward the end of his great ministry, Nephi taught, "If ye would hearken unto the Spirit which teacheth a man to pray ye would know that ye must pray; for the evil spirit teacheth not a man to pray, but teacheth him that he must not pray."

The evil one is not just leaving us alone, hoping we won't pray. He is trying to *stop* us from praying. I think about this sometimes when I don't feel that I want to pray. I can easily guess who is trying to convince me that I should not pray. President Brigham Young said, "Were I to draw a distinction in all the duties that are required of the children of men from first to last I would place first and foremost the duty of seeking unto the Lord our God until we open the path of communication from heaven to earth, from God to our own souls. Keep every avenue of your hearts clean and pure before him." (*Discourses of Brigham Young* [Salt Lake City: Deseret Book, 1954], 44.)

What Is Prayer?

What is prayer? I like looking in the Bible Dictionary. It wasn't until the last ten or fifteen years that I started using it more. It's back there past our "Tropical" Guide, and it contains some wonderful things about prayer. Here are some examples: "As soon as we learn the true relationship in which we stand toward God (namely, God is our Father, and we are his children), then at once prayer becomes natural and instinctive on our part." Isn't that beautiful? *Natural and instinctive.* "Many of the so-called difficulties about prayer arise from forgetting this relationship.

"Prayer is the act by which the will of the Father and the will of the child are brought into correspondence with each other." That is powerful.

"The object of prayer is not to change the will of God, but to secure for ourselves and for others blessings that God is already willing to grant, but that are made conditional on our asking for them." That's all he asks—that we ask.

"Blessings require some work or effort on our part before we can obtain them. Prayer is a form of work, and is an appointed means for obtaining the highest of all blessings." Prayer is a commandment, yes, but it is also one of the sweetest blessings in our lives here on earth.

Too often in my life prayer has been something I *have* to do and not something that I consider a blessing or enjoy and look forward to. President Marion G. Romney said, "There isn't any commandment from the Lord that is repeated more often than the commandment to pray to the Lord. Prayer is the key that opens the door to the Spirit of the Lord." (Taipei Taiwan Area Conference, 1975, 7.) May I emphasize that: "Prayer is the key that opens the door to the Spirit."

Prayer has been an important part of gospel living right from the beginning. An angel told Eve and Adam that they should repent and call upon God in the name of the Son. (See Moses 5:8.) All through the scriptures there are admonitions about and examples of the importance of prayer. In Alma 37:37, Alma Junior spoke to his son Helaman. We are familiar with this verse, but there is a part of it I want to emphasize. He said, "Counsel with the Lord in all thy doings, and he will direct thee for good; yea, when thou liest down at night lie down unto the Lord, that he may watch over you in your sleep; and when thou risest in the morning let thy heart be full of thanks unto God; and if ye do these things, ye shall be lifted up at the last day."

The part I want to emphasize is, "When thou risest in the morning let thy heart be full of thanks unto God." I am a morning person now, but I haven't always been. Earlier in my life, I don't know if I could have arisen in the morning with my heart full of thanks. I usually arise thinking, "What do I have to do today?" But it could make a difference in our whole day if we were to arise in the morning with a heart full of thanks to God.

What if we don't feel like praying? Brigham Young said, "It matters not whether you or I feel like praying, when the time comes to pray, pray. If we do not feel like it we should pray till we do. And if there is a heavy storm coming on or our hay is likely to be wet, let it come." (*Discourses of Brigham Young,* 44.) We need to find a way to make prayer a part of our lives. "We should live so as to deem it one of the greatest privileges accorded to us," said Brigham Young, "for were it not for the efficacy of prayer, what would have become of us both as a people and as individuals?" (*Discourses of Brigham Young,* 43.) And I might add, what will become of us if we don't pray as individuals and as a people?

Prayer and Work

Have you ever been kneeling down by your bed, praying—and all of a sudden you're jerked awake, and there is dry drool on your face, and your hair is matted to your head, and you can't remember if you finished your prayer? That is so embarrassing. You think, "Should I finish again? What should I do?" Or have you ever been praying and all of a sudden you realize you're daydreaming? Maybe you're singing a song or you're thinking about something else.

When that has happened to me I have imagined that Heavenly Father has a secretary—I don't know that he does, but if he does, he says to her, "If she comes back, let me know, because we were talking and all of a sudden she just started humming this song from the '50s." As it says in the Bible Dictionary, prayer is a form of work. It takes work to focus on your prayer.

Someone said we should pray as if everything depended on God and then work as if everything depended on us. Sister Pat Holland shared this profound thought at a BYU women's conference several years ago: "[Prayer] ought not to seem just a convenient and contrived miracle. No, if we are to search for real light and eternal certainties, we have to pray as the ancients prayed. We are women now, not children, and we are expected to pray with maturity. The words most often used to describe urgent, prayerful labor are *wrestle, plead, cry,* and *hunger.* In some sense, prayer may be the hardest work we will ever be engaged in, and perhaps it should be. We sing, 'Prayer is the soul's sincere desire,' our most basic declaration that we have no other God before us. It is our most pivotal protection against overinvolvement in worldly things and becoming so absorbed with possessions and privilege and honors and status that we no longer desire to undertake the search for our soul." ("'Many Things . . . One Thing,'" in *The Best of Women's Conference* [Salt Lake City: Bookcraft, 2000], 197.)

So we pray earnestly, and then we go to work to enable what we pray for to come to pass in our lives.

Elder Richard L. Evans had a wonderful way of expressing this idea. "It is not the usual purpose of prayer," he said, "to serve us like Aladdin's lamp, to bring us ease without effort. Prayer is not a matter of asking only. Often the purpose of prayer is to give us strength to do what needs to be done, wisdom to see the way to solve our own problems, and the ability to do our best in our tasks." (*The Man and the Message* [Salt Lake City: Bookcraft, 1973], 289.)

Amulek was Alma's missionary companion in teaching the Zoramites. That was a very hard mission. In Alma 34, Amulek gives a whole list of ways and reasons to pray—in your fields, in your closets, and so forth. And then in Alma 34:28 he teaches the connection between praying and doing: "And now behold, my beloved brethren, I say unto you, do not suppose that this is all; for after ye have done all these things, if ye turn away the needy, and the naked, and visit not the sick and afflicted, and impart of your substance, if ye have, to those who stand in need—I say unto you, if ye do not any of these things, behold, your prayer is vain, and availeth you nothing, and ye are as hypocrites who do deny the faith."

Those are pretty strong words from Amulek. I have wondered if sometimes we deny the faith of those who count on us. They have faith that we—or someone—will be an instrument in God's hands to reach out to them in their need, in their nakedness, or their sickness or affliction.

A Magic Wand

Are prayers answered? Remember my experience with finding my scriptures? Not all of my prayers have been answered that way. For example, when I was a little girl I lived in a wonderful neighborhood—and then Sharon moved in. She was a year older and a lot bigger than I, and she really interrupted my life. She began to get in my face, and she wouldn't let me do things the way I had ordinarily done things. I had had the run of the neighborhood—I could pretty much do what I wanted when I wanted. The only ones I couldn't beat up on were the parents.

But then there was Sharon. She became such an annoyance that I decided to get rid of her. We didn't have TV yet, so I didn't know all the possible ways that I could eliminate Sharon. I thought and thought about it, but couldn't come up with a good idea. Then one day I was looking at one of our wonderful fairy-tale books with the beautiful illustrations. On one page there was a fairy godmother with a magic wand. She went "poof!" with the magic wand and stars shot out in every direction. On the next page everything was changed, and there was no evidence of what she had done. That was just what I was looking for. I knew that if you killed someone and you left evidence you went to prison. I did not want to go to prison. I just wanted to rid my life of Sharon.

Where could I get a magic wand? I went downtown and walked up and down Main Street, checking all the stores. I didn't ask any of the storekeepers, "Do you have magic wands?" because I knew that once Sharon was gone the FBI would come and ask all these storekeepers if there was anybody asking about a magic wand. And they would answer, "Oh, yes, there was that little Edmunds kid from First West. She was in here not days before Sharon disappeared." So I just looked around, but couldn't find one.

Then it struck me: Pray! Heavenly Father could give me a magic wand! I did have the sense to know that it would be best if I had a good day before I asked him. So for an entire day I tried to be good. I was nice to all my brothers and sisters, my parents, the neighbors. I spent a lot of time in my room because it was dangerous to go out and mingle and still try to be good.

That evening I approached my Heavenly Father. First I asked him if he had noticed how nice I had been that day. And then I asked him for a magic wand. I didn't tell him what it was for. (I might be dumb, but I'm not stupid!) At this point I may have been a little mixed up about Santa and Heavenly Father because I was imagining workshops and elves making a magic wand. I figured it would take them a while, so I waited a few days.

And then I began to search in earnest for my magic wand, all the time snickering whenever I saw Sharon. "Huh-huh-huh. She has no idea what's going to happen to her. Poof!" Well, I never found the wand. I thought for a while that my younger sister, Charlotte, had found it and she was going to eliminate *me,* so I looked through all her stuff. No wand.

And then something inside of me brought me to the realization that I wasn't getting my magic wand. Two scriptures explain what I needed to understand, and sometimes still don't understand as well as I should. The first contains the Savior's words in 3 Nephi

18:20: "And whatsoever ye shall ask the Father in my name, which is right"—DING!—"believing that ye shall receive, behold it shall be given unto you." I didn't really understand yet that what you're asking for needs to be right before the Lord.

The other reference is Moroni 7:26, the words of Moroni's father, Mormon, toward the end of the Book of Mormon. "And as surely as Christ liveth he spake these words unto our fathers, saying: Whatsoever thing ye shall ask the Father in my name, which is good, in faith believing that ye shall receive, behold, it shall be done unto you."

In this verse the words are "which is good." We need to ask for that which is *right* and which is *good*. No wonder prayer is a form of work. We have to think it through: "Is this right? Is this good?" And no wonder prophets sometimes pray about *what to pray for*.

King Benjamin also teaches that we must pray only for what is right. (See Mosiah 4:21.) And Doctrine and Covenants 88:64 explains that we must ask only for things that are "expedient" for us. Sometimes I still pray for magic wands. Not literally, of course, but sometimes I'm so sure, I'm so positive, that something needs to be a certain way.

Answers

So we return to the question: Are prayers answered? I am convinced that God hears, understands, and responds to every single earnest, sincere prayer. I feel with all my heart that he does. One example of his invitation to come close to him is in Doctrine and Covenants 88:63: "Draw near unto me and I will draw near unto you; seek me diligently and ye shall find me; ask, and ye shall receive; knock, and it shall be opened unto you."

That verse reminds us of what the Bible Dictionary teaches: There are blessings he wants to give us, and he wants us to ask, to knock, to seek. That's all. Most of the time when I have felt my prayers were not answered, it was because the answer wasn't what I wanted. I may have said that he didn't answer my prayer. But he may have said "No" or "Maybe" or "Not yet" or "I'll consider it," rather than what I wanted to hear.

President David O. McKay taught, "I cherish as one of the dearest experiences of life the knowledge that God hears the prayer of faith. It is true that the answers to our prayers may not always come as direct and at the time, nor in the manner, we anticipate; but they do come." (In Conference Report, April 1969, 153.)

I know that is true. Answers do come. It takes complete trust in our Heavenly Father to turn things over to him and to say—what are those four words that are sometimes so hard to say?—*Thy will be done.* Have you ever had a really tough time saying that? I think many of us have. We know we're supposed to say it. Sometimes I say it, and then I add a little P.S.: *Thy will be done—but please consider the things I've shared with you.*

One of my friends was going through a very difficult experience. He said, "I talked to the Lord, and I gave him five excellent options: *A, B, C, D,* and *E.* I said, 'Now *A* and *B* would be fine, or all of the above, or *D.*'" Then he paused and said, "The Lord chose *Q.*"

That's a perfect way to describe the way things sometimes happen. Believing in the phrase "thy will be done" is so important. I was talking to somebody one time about saying to the Lord, "Thy will be done." The person said, "Well, then, that cancels out your prayer." But we understand that it doesn't do that at all. It is an acknowledgment that we know that he sees so much more than we can see and that he understands everything.

I know I'm not the only one who has wondered about miracles and answers to prayers and why it seems that some people receive a "yes" and other people don't. For example, why is one child spared and another child taken, when all those surrounding both of those little children prayed so hard? I know I lack wisdom; I lack experience. How do we keep from sometimes doubting our faith or our worthiness? How do we keep from sometimes doubting that the Lord loves us? How do we keep from becoming bitter or angry or separated from God if we feel that something unfair has happened? I'm convinced that there will be accountability for all that happens in this world. It will catch some off guard who thought they had persecuted, sinned, abused, and blasphemed in secret. There are times when I forget that God really does have an eternal perspective and he can see the whole picture.

He loves us. He knows us so well, and he knows the future. He knows what's going to happen. I've thought a lot about these things. I don't have all the answers, but I want to share something that happened to me. There have been times in testimony meeting when someone shared with deep conviction a miracle that had happened to them or their family—and in the same congregation were others who had prayed equally diligently, and their miracle didn't happen.

Things like that make you wonder. A cousin of mine was thirty-eight years old with six children. She had cancer, and she wanted to stay and raise her children. We prayed so hard, and there were priesthood blessings and a lot of fasting and prayer, and she was taken home.

I was pondering this one day when it came into my mind that there are many examples in the scriptures of prayers answered and prayers not answered. And that's not even really what I mean— that's the "earthling" way of looking at it. What I mean is that there are examples of times when some prayers were answered positively right away, and others didn't seem to be.

We learn about two prophets in the Book of Mormon who had rebellious sons. One was named Alma. He had a son named Alma who was very wicked—he even seemed anti-father, anti-Alma Senior. He went about with his friends trying to destroy everything that his father was trying to build. Alma Senior fasted and prayed long and hard for his son, and I'm sure his mother and many others did as well. You know what happened. Alma Junior and his friends were visited by an angel and had an experience that changed their hearts and their lives. They became some of the most powerful missionaries in history. Alma Junior became a great prophet and chief judge and progenitor of an equally great son and grandson and great-grandson. His line became very important in the Book of Mormon.

Another prophet, Lehi, also had a wicked son, whose name was Laman. Laman became anti-church and anti-father—he even tried to kill his father. He was also visited by an angel, but it didn't seem to have a lasting effect on him. He became the progenitor of a mostly wicked line of people in the Book of Mormon.

The Spirit whispered questions to my mind. Both prophets prayed and fasted for their sons and did everything they could to persuade them to be good and to believe in Christ. Was Alma Senior more faithful than Lehi? I don't think so. Lehi's life seems to be just as faithful as Alma's. Was he more obedient? No—Lehi left everything and went into the wilderness as he had been commanded to do. (In that little poignant verse, "My father dwelt in a tent" (1 Nephi 2:15), I think Nephi was saying, "You should have seen the difference between this tent and where we lived in Jerusalem!") Was Alma Senior more worthy? No. Did God love him more? Absolutely not. Did he pray with greater faith? I don't think so.

Do you see where that little lesson took me? It took me back to saying that there are a lot of things I don't understand—but that it is still important to pray as hard as we can, and then leave things in the hands of our Heavenly Father. President Spencer W. Kimball said, "Prayers are not always answered as we wish them to be. Even the Redeemer's prayer in Gethsemane was answered in the negative. He prayed that the bitter cup of sorrow, pain, and mortal life termination could pass, but the answer was a 'no' answer." (*Teachings of Spencer W. Kimball* [Salt Lake City: Bookcraft, 1982], 124.)

Some Questions and Answers about Prayer

How do we get answers to our prayers? Someone has said that God doesn't send thunder when a still small voice can be heard. Perhaps your experience has been like mine and some of your answers have been quiet and peaceful. Perhaps an answer to a prayer came at a time you would not have expected or anticipated it. Elder Bruce R. McConkie said, "It is not, never has been, and never will be the desire and purpose of the Lord, however much we seek him in prayer, to answer all our problems and concerns without struggle and effort on our part." ("Why the Lord Ordained Prayer," *Ensign,* Jan. 1976, 11.) A man named Henry Ward Beecher said, "It is not well for a man to pray cream and live skim milk." (Quoted by Howard W. Hunter, "Hallowed Be Thy Name," *Ensign,* Nov. 1977, 52.) I like that thought.

What should we pray for? Alma Junior made a wonderful comment about this in Alma 7:23: "[Ask] for whatsoever things ye stand in need, both spiritual and temporal; always returning thanks unto God for whatsoever things ye do receive." That part I sometimes forget. I pray and pray, and receive my answer, and I forget to say thank you.

President Kimball has pointed out the importance—and the privilege—of praying for forgiveness. He quoted Enos, who is a good example of a lot of things about prayer, including the fact that it is a form of work: "All the day long did I cry unto him." (Enos 1:4.) Then President Kimball commented: "Here is no casual prayer, no worn phrases. All the day long with seconds turning into minutes and minutes into hours and hours, but when the sun had set relief had still not come. For repentance is not a single act nor forgiveness an unearned gift. So precious to him was communication with and approval of his Redeemer that his determined soul pressed on. 'Yea, and when the night came I did still raise my voice high that it reached the heavens.'"

President Kimball continued: "Could the Redeemer resist such determined imploring? How many have thus persisted? How many with or without serious transgression have ever prayed all day and into the night? How many have ever wept and prayed for ten hours? For five hours? For one? For thirty minutes? For ten? Our praying is usually measured in seconds and yet with a heavy debt to pay we still expect forgiveness for our sins. We offer pennies to pay the debt of thousands of dollars." (*Faith Precedes the Miracle* [Salt Lake City: Deseret Book, 1972], 211.)

Sometimes the Lord chastised those who forgot to talk to him. In the book of Ether we read that it was for about three hours that the Lord visited with the brother of Jared and reminded him that he hadn't prayed in a while.

Why do we use words such as "thee," "thou," "thy," and "thine"? These are a little tricky if you haven't grown up using them. A wonderful article by Elder Dallin H. Oaks in the May 1993 *Ensign* addresses using prayer language. "When we go to worship in a temple or a church," he reminded us, "we put aside our working clothes and dress ourselves in something better. This change of clothing is a mark of respect. Similarly, when we address our Heavenly Father, we should put aside our working words and

47

clothe our prayers in special language of reverence and respect. . . . In our prayers we use language that is dignified and different." (pp. 15, 16.) These words *thee, thy, thou* and *thine* are intimate as well as respectful words.

How can we increase our enjoyment of communication with our Heavenly Father? One day I was writing down ideas of how to make our prayers more meaningful. I wrote, "Be real," and then, "Pretend Heavenly Father is listening." I burst out laughing—because of course he is listening! What I meant is that we can *imagine* that we actually are speaking to him face to face, and we can imagine him listening to us, and loving us. I think that too many times we imagine him angry with us or disappointed in us, or looking down from some heavenly office, saying, "Oh, I saw that. Put a black mark by her name." It's important that we remember how much he loves us, and that we picture him loving us and understanding everything that we share with him.

Matthew 6:7 includes a good reminder: "But when ye pray, use not vain repetitions, as the heathen do." I don't want to be a heathen when I pray. I want to be Heavenly Father's child. I want to be able to communicate with him freely and openly and honestly and share whatever is in my heart. I saw a bumper sticker that read, "Prayer—the next best thing to being there." I thought that perhaps another bumper sticker could say, "Prayer is being there."

What about listening? Do you ever forget to listen when you pray? Sometimes I do. I just go on, "Yackety-yackety-yackety," and I might even be thinking that I have to hurry and get back to what I was doing. But we ought not to hurry through our prayers. We need to give Heavenly Father a chance to communicate with us. When we are talking to him as his little children, asking questions, sharing feelings and experiences, it is the ideal time for him to bring some prompting or reminder or idea into our minds.

Have you ever written down some of those impressions? They are very personal and very sacred. They are not the kind of thing that you share in a testimony meeting or at a family reunion. They are just for you and may give a wonderful sense of direction just when you need it.

Strengthening Our Prayers

There are a number of things we can do to strengthen our prayers. One thing that helps me to be ready to pray is to *sing a hymn* before I begin. I have a habit of reading a hymn or two every day. Sometimes I can't stand to read just one and I read two or three. There are some really beautiful hymns that we don't often sing. And sometimes we sing the familiar ones, such as "We Thank Thee, O God, for a Prophet," or "How Firm a Foundation," without thinking about the words. Singing or reading the words of a hymn really brings the Spirit.

We need to *find opportunities to pray out loud*. When I was a teenager, we had a boxer dog who was my prayer buddy. There were no homes east of us, and she and I would walk up the street into the foothills. She would guard me from Bigfoot or mountain lions or whatever might be a threat—although I think the biggest thing up there is maybe a squirrel. While she was on guard I would pray out loud. Those are wonderful times when you can pray out loud.

Add another prayer to your day. Amulek advised us to pray morning, midday, and evening. (See Alma 34:21.) If you usually pray in the morning and in the evening, perhaps you might add a prayer somewhere in the middle of the day. Another thing to do is add a minute to your prayer. When I do this it really makes a difference in my personal prayers. I am ready to conclude my prayer and then I remember that I'm going to add one minute. I tell the Lord that

I don't want to close yet, and for one more minute—and often it's more than one minute—I pour out some deeper feelings and thoughts. It becomes one of the sweetest parts of the prayer. (This probably wasn't my idea so feel free to borrow it.)

Pray for others specifically by name, even if they're listening. As a child I loved hearing my parents pray for me. (I thought it was so sweet that they'd pray that I wouldn't hurt anyone that day, or that I'd be nice.) Pray for Church leaders, men and women. Pray for people from faraway places with strange-sounding names. Lately we've been praying for people in Afghanistan—a name we probably couldn't pronounce not too long ago. And isn't Heavenly Father a genius to ask us to pray for our enemies? "Enemy" doesn't necessarily mean someone who wants to go to war with you. It may mean someone who has not been very nice to you lately. When you pray for them by name, the "enemy" part goes away. The anger seems to melt.

To pray better, live better—and to live better, pray better. (I probably saw that on a bumper sticker, too.) There is a wonderful thought in James 5:16: "The effectual fervent prayer of a righteous man availeth much." As we do good and are good, our prayers can be a wonderful experience.

We need to *offer "thank you" prayers.* One stake president invited his stake to find a day and time when they didn't have to be in a hurry and to "count [their] many blessings; name them one by one." (*Hymns,* no. 241.) He said to ponder specific things that you feel thankful for—everything you can think of—and then specifically thank the Lord for those things in prayer. Following that experience, he said, you can then begin thinking of things you forgot to include in your prayer, other things for which you are grateful, and imagine what your life would be like without those things. Then thank him for those.

I did that one day. It took me about an hour. (It should have taken a lot longer.) I was so specific in things that I was grateful for—and then it amazed me that one of the things I forgot to thank him for was water. Because of experiences I have had when water wasn't available, or the water wasn't safe, or I had a canteen that ran out halfway up the hike to Mount Timpanogos, water means a lot to me. Water is a precious thing that I often thank Heavenly Father for. But in that long "thank you" prayer that day I forgot to include water. I imagined what my life would be like without water—of course I would perish. Can you think of two or three things you'd like to thank Heavenly Father for that you haven't included in your prayer for a while?

Seek the peace of prayer. I love the phrase, "O, how praying rests the weary!" (*Hymns,* no. 31.) Sister Elaine Jack said a friend of hers had a poster above her sink with the following message: "At night I turn all my problems over to Heavenly Father. He's going to be up all night anyway." What a wonderful thing it is to know that he will watch over us even as we sleep.

Take your questions to the Lord. The book of James also contains that wonderful scripture that compelled Joseph Smith to pray for an answer: "If any of you lack wisdom, let him ask of God, that giveth to all men liberally, and upbraideth not; and it shall be given him. But let him ask in faith, nothing wavering." (James 1:5–6.) If someone or some circumstance is causing you to doubt or to question or to be troubled or afraid, talk to the Lord about it. Share it with him. Some may say, "He knows all our thoughts already—why do we need to voice them?" Because sometimes in the process of trying to put our questions and our concerns into words, things become clearer and we see them in a different light. The very sharing of what's in our hearts helps us to know that he understands.

We might ask specific questions. Is there something he wants us to do? Is there something he wants us to stop doing? Is there someone who needs us? We can share with Heavenly Father what we know to be true. We might even bear our testimonies to him—what a wonderful thing that would be to share with him.

Pray as a family. Family prayer has been an important part of my family life. I mentioned how I loved hearing my parents pray for me when I was a child. In their later years they would pray sitting at the kitchen table. They were no longer able to get up from a kneeling position and couldn't help each other up, so they would sit and hold hands and take turns praying.

On December 28, 1997, we had our last family prayer with my dad on this earth. It was time for him to go home. He knew it, and we knew it. We gathered around his bed at the hospital and prayed together. It was an incredible experience to ask Heavenly Father to gently and kindly take him home. I don't know how we could have done that if we hadn't known something about where he was going.

A final suggestion is to *remember the Savior's prayer in Gethsemane.* We will likely never fully comprehend what happened there. As an earthling, I often think more about the physical pain of the crucifixion because I can't even stand a paper cut. I get upset about little things like that so it's hard to imagine nails being driven through his hands and his feet. But the pain he suffered in the Garden was something beyond our comprehension. He earned the right to be our advocate, our mediator. He pleads with the Father on our behalf. This is why we pray in his name. I hope we will not hurry over that part of our prayer and forget what it means. Every time we pray, may we say his name carefully and meaningfully, and with some comprehension of what he has done for us.

First Prayers

What if we're new at this? What if we or someone we know doesn't really know how to pray or hasn't prayed for a long time or isn't sure what prayer is all about? President Joseph F. Smith said, "It is not such a difficult thing to learn how to pray. It is not the words we use particularly that constitute prayer. True faithful earnest prayer consists more in the feeling that rises from the heart and from the inward desire of our spirits to supplicate the Lord in humility and in faith that we may receive his blessings. It matters not how simple the words may be if our desires are genuine and we come before the Lord with a broken heart and a contrite spirit to ask him for that which we need." (In Conference Report, Oct. 1969, 71–72.) It doesn't matter how simple the words are. The feelings of our heart are what make a true, real prayer.

It is such a tender and holy thing to hear someone's first prayer. It is like listening to a little child, no matter what age the person is. Missionaries love this part of their work. I think of Aaron listening to King Lamoni's father's first prayer: "If there is a God, and if thou art God, I want to know thee. I will give away all my sins to know thee." (See Alma 22:18.) What a tender thing for Aaron to hear.

When I was a missionary in the Philippines, my companion and I taught a man by the name of Brother Ocampo. He was hesitant to let us in because he didn't speak English very well. (This was in the days before missionaries were taught the languages of the Philippines.) We taught him as simply as we knew how. We taught him to pray in four simple steps: We address our Heavenly Father. We thank him for our blessings. We ask him for what we need. We close in the name of Jesus Christ.

Each time we visited him we asked him to choose someone to offer the opening and closing prayers. He would offer one of the prayers and ask my companion or me to offer the other one. Because we were sure we had taught him well, we knew he was offering wonderful prayers—he prayed in his own language and we didn't understand all the words, but we felt good feelings. We would ask, "Have you been praying, Brother Ocampo?"

"Oh, yes, sisters," he would reply, "I pray every day."

"And do you feel your prayers being heard and answered?"

"Oh, yes, sisters, he's listening to me."

After several weeks Brother Ocampo was baptized. At a sacrament meeting shortly after his baptism, the branch president asked if Brother Ocampo would offer the closing prayer—and he said no. This puzzled us, because we knew he prayed all the time. After the meeting he asked us to come to his place. After we arrived we visited for a few minutes, and it was obvious that there was something on his mind. He said, "Sisters, I want to pray the way you pray."

Brother Ocampo, as it turned out, had not understood what we had thought was an excellent lesson on prayer. This sixty-five-year-old man had selected six or seven favorite memorized prayers and had said those same things over and over. In his prayers, he had never mentioned Joseph Smith, the Book of Mormon, the Atonement, and the restored Church—although he had gained a testimony of those very things and had been baptized! Now he was asking us, "Teach me to pray the way you pray."

We tried again to teach him about prayer—and he certainly taught us more that day than we taught him. He said, "Oh, sisters, this is very beautiful, no?"

We said, "Oh, yes, Brother Ocampo, it is."

"Can I really just talk to him? Can I say anything I want to say?"

"Yes, yes, you can!"

Finally, he said, "Can we pray now, sisters?"

We said, "Of course we can. We can pray any time."

So we knelt together and he said, "I'll be the one to pray. I'm going to try to pray in English because then when I make mistakes you can correct them later. You can tell me what I said wrong." Would he make any mistakes? Of course not.

One of the first things he taught us that day was not to be in a hurry. We knelt together and he waited a long time to begin. We were already weeping because it was the first time that he was going to talk to his Heavenly Father just from his heart and say anything he wanted to say, and he knew it. He also knew Heavenly Father would be listening.

After a time he began, "Oh, Heavenly Father," and then he started to cry. We were all weeping together. He had worked hard to prepare some thoughts and feelings in English. He said a few words and then stopped. "Sisters?"

"Yes?"

"If I am slow, will he wait?"

"Oh, yes, he'll wait. Don't worry, he'll wait."

He was teaching us, reminding us. He prayed a little more, then said, "Sisters?"

"Yes?"

"I can say anything?"

"Anything."

He said another sentence or two. "Sisters?"

"Yes?"

"This is very beautiful, no?"

"Yes, Brother Ocampo, this is so beautiful."

Then he said, "Sisters?"

"Yes?"

"Does he know Tagalog? Does he know my language?"

This was interesting for me because when I read the scriptures,

I imagine Heavenly Father and the Savior saying everything in English. I know they know *my* language, so of course they know all of the others. It was so good to be able to honestly say, "Yes, he knows Tagalog."

Brother Ocampo said, "Then I can finish in my own language? I can say anything I want?"

"Yes." Then he poured out his heart to Heavenly Father. Just for a moment part of me thought, "Oh-oh, I wonder what he's saying." Then the Spirit said to me, "It's okay, Edmunds, just settle down. He's not praying to you."

What a wonderful thing prayer is. Heavenly Father understood every single feeling of Brother Ocampo's heart. Even though Brother Ocampo didn't know the words to say, Heavenly Father knew what he wanted to express. And that is true of every prayer that you offer. He knows what you're trying to say. He knows that you want to be good and to choose the right. He knows that. May prayer be our soul's sincere desire and one of the most enjoyable blessings we experience on this earth.

The Intimate
Touch of Prayer

TRUMAN G. MADSEN

A LL OF US NEED deeper understanding in prayer. All of us reach. All of us speak. But none of us have perfected the process and all of us need encouragement. Here is a portrait of the prayer life of the Prophet Joseph Smith. I'm convinced that as we feel our way into his life we will receive glimpses that are more vivid and helpful than if we simply read statements about what we ought to do—the Prophet's life gives us clear insight into what we can do.

There is a letter in the Prophet's handwriting written in 1832—only a few months after one of the most remarkable revelations he received. The record of that revelation is now section 46 of the Doctrine and Covenants. Joseph is writing to his wife, Emma.

"My situation is a very unpleasant one, although I will endeavor to be contented, the Lord assisting me. I have visited a grove which is just back of the town, almost every day, where I can be secluded from the eyes of any mortal, and there give vent to all the feelings of my heart in meditation and prayers. I have called to mind all the past moments of my life, and am left to mourn and shed tears of sorrow for my folly in suffering the adversary of my soul to have so much power over me, as he has had in times past. But God is merciful and has forgiven my sins, and I rejoice that he sendeth forth His Comforter unto as many as believe and humble themselves before Him." (Joseph Smith, in Dean Jessee, *Personal Writings of Joseph Smith* [Salt Lake City: Deseret Book, 1984, 238; Spelling and punctuation standardized.)

Now, that one paragraph is enough to tell us that he was struggling—blessed and magnified though he was—just as we are struggling with the weight of life, with the difficulties and weaknesses that are in us, and with the constant desire to receive of the Lord.

Some have asked in my hearing, "How is it that the Prophet Joseph Smith, age fourteen, could go into a grove, never before having prayed vocally (according to his own account, implying that he had prayed before in his heart), and that in that first prayer he received great and marvelous blessings—transcendent blessings? Does that mean that he simply had far greater faith than any of the rest of us?"

One possible response to that is that the answer the Prophet Joseph Smith received wasn't just to his own prayer. I submit that it was to the prayers of literally millions, maybe those even beyond the veil who had been seeking and reaching for generations for the restoration of the gospel and the reestablishment of the kingdom of God on the earth. That suggests that you and I do not pray alone. We pray as part of a great modern movement, and we are united in that very process. I sometimes think that therefore we have some advantages that are not shared by others who have not yet found the gospel, found the authorities and gifts and blessings of the Holy Ghost, and found the crowning blessing of the priesthood.

Let me ask some elementary questions about Joseph Smith's prayer life to help us feel even closer to him, as his experience overlaps our own. Did the Prophet pray long or short? Was he, as we judge prayers, inclined to multiply words or was he inclined to be brief? The answer to that question is yes. There were times when the Prophet prayed briefly; there also were times when he stayed on his knees in prayer for a long time. Of the first, an example is an experience at Kirtland. The table has been set, and there is little to eat. He stands at the table and says, "Lord, we thank thee for this johnnycake and ask thee to send us something better. Amen." Shortly, someone knocks on the door, and there stands a man with a ham and some flour. The Prophet jumps to his feet and says to Emma, "I knew the Lord would answer my prayer." Well, that's a telegram prayer—that's very brief. (See Truman G. Madsen, *Joseph Smith* [Salt Lake City: Bookcraft, 1989], 32.)

On the other hand Mary Elizabeth Rollins Lightner, a convert to the Church, only fourteen years of age at the time of the experience, describes coming with her mother to the Prophet's home, sharing in a small meeting where he set up a box or two and put a board across them to make room for people to sit. Now he spoke with great power. One of her comments is that his face, to her at least, "turned so white, he seemed perfectly transparent." A great outpouring of the Spirit. But then he asked them to kneel. And he prayed. Such a prayer, she says, "I never heard before or since." So much did this prolong the meeting that some on the hard floor stood up, rubbed their knees a bit, and then knelt down again. It was long. (See Hyrum L. Andrus and Helen Mae Andrus, *They Knew the Prophet* [Salt Lake City: Bookcraft, 1974], 23–24.)

Did the Prophet address the Lord as "Father," or did he have a special manner of address? Most frequently, the Prophet prayed "Our Father" or simply, "Father," or "O Lord," and was not inclined, as are some in our midst, to add adjectives and flowery phrases to that. I'm not saying that making such additions is wrong, but I note that he was intimate in prayer and that a simple "Father" was sufficient.

In counseling some missionaries he once said, "Make short prayers and short sermons." And he said on another occasion, "Be plain and simple, and ask for what you want, just like you would go to a neighbor and say, 'I want to borrow your horse to go to the mill.'" (See Andrus and Andrus, *They Knew the Prophet,* 100.) That's plain. That's simple. And that's honest. So were his prayers.

There were times in sacred circumstances when the Prophet prayed in a formal way. I have in mind especially the unique situation of dedicating temples. Some people were upset and even left the Church through the experiences of the temple, either because so little occurred in their own experience or because so much did. The Prophet read the dedicatory prayer for the Kirtland Temple and announced that it had been given him by revelation. We have it recorded in section 109 of the Doctrine and Covenants. That prayer has become the model, the archetype, if you will, for all subsequent temple dedication prayers. Some members were disturbed at that. First of all, they'd been taught that we don't have set prayers in our midst. The truth is that we have some. The Lord has not permitted us to modify the sacramental prayers—not by one word. They are set. And so also with the baptismal prayer.

Second, they were troubled that here was a man who had apparently been given these words to say by the Lord to whom he was to say them. That struck them as circular. But the Prophet elsewhere has taught us that, as President J. Reuben Clark put it, one of the things we should most often pray for is to know what we should most often pray for. At least half of the prayer process is our bringing our souls into receptivity so that we know what we ought to pray; we listen. There are direct statements in modern revelation, for example, about being given all things:

"He that is ordained of God and sent forth, the same is appointed to be the greatest, notwithstanding he is the least and the servant of all.

"Wherefore, he is possessor of all things; for all things are subject unto him, both in heaven and on the earth, the life and the light, the Spirit and the power. . . .

"But no man is possessor of all things except he be purified and cleansed from all sin.

"And if ye are purified and cleansed from all sin, ye shall ask whatsoever you will in the name of Jesus and it shall be done."

Then: "But know this, it shall be given you what you shall ask." (D&C 50:26–30.) A sensitive, developing, spiritual-minded person becomes more and more attentive and responsive to the Spirit and is able, therefore, to pray as the Prophet did. The Lord also said: "He that asketh in the Spirit asketh according to the will of God; wherefore it is done even as he asketh." (D&C 46:30.) Thus we ought to follow the Prophet's lead, to listen and to pray with the Spirit; then the Spirit will prompt us both as to how we should pray and what we should say as we pray.

I've asked myself, "Did the Prophet sometimes pray for things never given or for guidance not allowed, or for privileges denied him?" He did. Like us, he sometimes struggled, and the Lord simply left that problem without solving it.

Two examples. The Prophet earnestly desired to know the time of the Savior's second coming. We've been taught no man knows the day nor the hour; but still, get a group of Latter-day Saints together, and after they admit that premise they say, "But, what do you think?" Well, the Prophet also wondered. He prayed very fervently to know, and the Lord's answer wasn't really an answer, except, "I won't tell you." It was: "Joseph, my son, if thou livest until thou art eighty-five years old, thou shalt see the face of the Son of Man; therefore let this suffice, and trouble me no more on this matter." (D&C 130:15.) Joseph first assumed that that meant Christ would come in fifty-six years, which would have been when he, Joseph, would become eighty-five. But he realized that wasn't what he'd been told. He'd been told that if he lived to be eighty-five he would see the face of the Lord, and that might mean after dying. So he put down the only conclusion he could come to. "I believe the coming of the Son of Man will not be any sooner than that time." (See D&C 130:14–17; see also Oliver Huntington, Diary, 129.)

God simply doesn't want us to know the timing of the Second Coming. He wants us to go on living, I suggest to you, as if it were going to happen tomorrow. Spiritually speaking, that's what He wants from us—to be prepared. As He says, "I come quickly." (Revelation 22:20.) But He also wants us to live our lives in a long-range way with inspiration and not in an unauthentic way, which some of our young people seem to follow. They say, "It's all going to blow up in our faces in five years, so why should I plan to go away to school?" That's not in keeping with the Lord's will.

On one occasion the Prophet was praying to know why our people had to suffer so in Missouri. A sorrowful letter he wrote them says, "He will not show [it] unto me." (Joseph Smith, *Teachings of the Prophet Joseph Smith,* comp. Joseph Fielding Smith [Salt Lake City: Deseret Book, 1938], 34.) There was at least one time earlier when he begged the Lord for what the Lord had told him He wouldn't give him. As we all do, the Prophet fell into the practice sometimes of saying, "Are you sure, Lord? Really, do you understand, Lord? I heard you, and the answer seems to be no, but are you sure?"

We remember the instance of Martin Harris. Twice the Prophet prayed asking for permission to lend Martin the manuscript. Twice the Lord said no. When the Prophet asked the third time, we might suppose he said or thought things like "But Lord, don't you understand, his wife is pushing him, Lord. What harm can it do? She needs to see something. She needs to have some reassurance." Well, there's a passage that says, "Seek not to counsel your God." (D&C 22:4.)

Mother Smith recalled how Martin came to the house, paced up and down in front, hesitant to open the door to tell the truth. The Prophet saw him out the window. Finally he entered the house. "Martin, have you lost . . . ?" (See Lucy Mack Smith, *History of Joseph Smith* [Salt Lake City: Bookcraft, 1958], 128–29.)

For two weeks, the Prophet could not be comforted. He felt he had betrayed the Lord. And no one can conceive the joy that entered his heart when the revelation came, "Behold, . . . repent of that which thou hast done . . . and thou . . . art again called to the work." (D&C 3:9–10.) He said thereafter, and I think this was a summary of his experience, "I made this my rule: When the Lord commands, do it." (Joseph Smith, *History of the Church,* ed. B. H. Roberts, 2d ed. 7 vols. [Salt Lake City: Deseret Book, 1948], 2:170.) Well, he learned that, but he learned the hard way.

Did the Prophet practice family prayer? The answer is yes. During one period of the Prophet's life Eliza R. Snow served as a kind of babysitter in his home, and she wrote a poem called "Narcissa to Narcissus." She described how she admired the Prophet in public—that she saw him for what he was. But when she was in his home and though, knowing his greatness, saw him, as she puts it, as humble and unassuming as a child, kneeling in family prayer, she could not withhold her heart, and she loved his soul. The phrase "Narcissa to Narcissus," I believe, suggests that to see him, as with the mythological lad who looked in the water and saw his own reflection, enabled her to see herself. She came to a deeper sense of prayer in beholding him.

A brother who had never met the Prophet or his family came and was about to knock on the door, but hesitated because he heard singing. Sister Emma was leading the family and the guests, who were always numerous, in a kind of preparatory worship service. And then the Prophet prayed. (See Andrus and Andrus, *They Knew the Prophet,* 147.) He prayed three times a day with his family. And though in our lives it's difficult to get together once and overlap everyone, I nevertheless recommend that principle. Morning, noon, and night they had a kind of family prayer—beautiful!

Joseph once said, citing the book of Daniel, "You must make yourselves acquainted with those men who like Daniel pray three times a day toward the House of the Lord." (Smith, *Teachings of the Prophet Joseph Smith,* 161.) What's the significance of facing the temple? Apparently it can help recall both the promises the Lord has made to us in the temple and the promises we have made to Him—covenants in the House of the Lord. When President Wilford Woodruff dedicated the Salt Lake Temple he offered a specific prayer that people who had there committed their lives to the Lord Jesus Christ and were now assailed with temptation or trouble but were unable to get to the temple to supplicate the Lord might face the temple as they prayed, and that the Lord would honor their prayers. (See N. B. Lundwall, *Temples of the Most High* [Salt Lake City: Bookcraft, 1968], 127.)

The Prophet, even in his own household, was temple-minded both at Kirtland and at Nauvoo. The temple has been designated by the Lord himself as "a house of prayer." (D&C 88:119.)

Did the Prophet pray when he was in desperate circumstances? Someone has said, intending it to be critical, that for some of us religion is like a spare tire—we never really put it on until we are in trouble. The Lord did indicate in a modern scripture that many in the day of peace and comparative well-being "esteemed lightly my counsel; but, in the day of their trouble, of necessity they feel after me." But He adds, "I will remember mercy." (D&C 101:8–9.)

Well, the Prophet was in circumstances that were hard and difficult. Brigham Young once said of him: "Joseph could not have been perfected . . . if he had received no persecution. If he had lived a thousand years, and led this people, and preached the Gospel without persecution, he would not have been perfected as well as he was at the age of thirty-nine years." (Brigham Young, *Journal of Discourses,* 26 vols. [Liverpool: F. D. Richards, 1855], 2:7.)

In one dramatic situation he was hauled out of his bed by four men one night and dragged on the ground, beaten, stripped, tarred and feathered. They attempted to poison him—because he clenched his teeth they failed to get the poison into his mouth, but it subsequently fell onto the grass and killed it. It was aqua fortis (nitric acid). A quack doctor who had his tools had threatened that he would emasculate the Prophet. He didn't. Even as they were at him like fiends, the Prophet vocally prayed to the Lord for deliverance. He did pray in extremity. My personal conviction is that the last words he spoke in this life were not, as some have supposed, a distress signal, but were a prayer: "O Lord, my God." These words, a few minutes later, Willard Richards repeated with hands uplifted as he thought of the condition of the Church in the loss of the Prophet.

Yes, Joseph prayed in extremity, but he also prayed in great gratitude. And here is another insight. He taught the Saints that they should practice virtue and holiness, but that they should give thanks unto God in the Spirit for whatsoever blessing they were blessed with. In my own life, years have gone by, I'm sure, when I have offered prayers yet never spent an entire prayer simply to thank the Lord. My prayers have always had an element of asking, asking, asking. But Joseph taught the Saints that if they would learn to be thankful in all things—simply be thankful—they would be made glorious, and their prayers would take on a deeper, richer spirit.

The sin of ingratitude is one of the things that prevent us from as rich a prayer life as he had. He seemed to have an innate and deep capacity for gratitude, even for the slightest favor, from the Lord as from his fellowmen. And I have wept at times while reading that in his journal he sometimes wrote a kind of prayer for a brother. "Bless Brother So-and-So, Father, who gave me $1.35 today to help with such-and-such a project." Even the smallest favor called forth his warmth and gratitude.

Was the Prophet effective in silent prayers, did he commend that or even command it? I note with interest eight different places where the Lord, through the Prophet, says, "pray always." That's a strong imperative. How can we? If "pray always" means vocally, then none of us do it—none of us can. But if "pray always" includes the kind of prayer that is from the heart and wordless, we're getting closer to a possibility. And if it means, even more profoundly, that we are to be in the spirit of prayer regardless of what we may be doing, then all of us can pray always.

The Prophet gave us a better rendering of a New Testament verse about prayer. It is Romans 8:26. The King James Version of the Bible has Paul saying (speaking of how the Spirit can assist us in prayer), "The Spirit itself maketh intercession for us with groanings which cannot be uttered." The Prophet's version is, "The Spirit maketh intercession for us with striving which cannot be expressed. (Smith, *Teachings of the Prophet Joseph Smith,* 278.) I think he is saying that when we have enough confidence in the discerning power of the Spirit, we stop worrying so much about the words we use and are concerned more simply to open up what is really deep in us—even things that we cannot find words for. Strivings are different than groanings—you can groan in discouragement and despondency and it can all be turned down instead of turned up, but strivings are upreaching. We can take our strivings—even those that we cannot express—and know that as we silently think and pour out our feelings, the Spirit will translate those and perfectly transmit them to the Lord. And in turn, the Spirit can respond from the Lord to us. A great confidence and a great freedom can come when we trust the Spirit for that.

The Prophet, as we know, became a learned man. He didn't begin so, but I occasionally wince a little when I hear people say, "Well, he was just an unlearned boy." How does one become learned? We say "go to school." What's a school? It's a place where there are teachers. Well, who were the Prophet's teachers? Not just the local schoolmarm or two in Palmyra. The Prophet Joseph Smith was taught face to face by some "minor" pedagogues like Moroni, Peter, James, and John, the ancient Apostles and prophets, and, if that weren't enough, the Father and the Son. It is not true to say that he was unlearned. He had the learning and wisdom of heaven. Who knows more about the epistles of Paul—professors who teach in graduate schools, or Paul?

We help ourselves in prayer by speaking aloud. It helps our minds stay on track. But there are advantages also to silent prayers and some kinds of mind wandering—letting the mind go in the direction that it seems to be impressed to go.

Now, just a word about the remarkable pattern the Prophet taught in the presence of priesthood brethren. This was a special kind of prayer circumstance in the Kirtland Temple. Here are his exact words: "I labored with each of these quorums [High Priests, Seventies, Elders] for some time to bring them to the order which God had shown to me, which is as follows: The first part to be spent in solemn prayer before God, without any talking or confusion." (I take that to mean solemn, silent prayer.) "And the conclusion with a sealing prayer by President Rigdon" (that is, one man would then pray vocally with and for the group), "when all the quorums were to shout with one accord a solemn hosanna to God and the Lamb with an Amen, Amen, and Amen."

Notice, in passing, that we're warned by the Lord against vain repetition, but we are not warned against repetition. There are things we not only can but should repeat in our lives. And it is not correct to suppose that after you say something once, you mustn't ever say it again. Vain repetition is the kind of vanity of repeating without genuine concern, just supposing that saying a thing over and over from the neck up without any feeling is acceptable. No. But the Hosanna Shout, itself, is a repetition—three times we say hosanna, hosanna, hosanna. And three times we say amen. To continue: "Then all take seats and lift up their hearts in silent prayer to God, and if any obtain a prophecy or vision, to rise and speak that all may be edified and rejoice together."

Now, that is a special set of instructions, but the spirit of it, it seems to me, applies even to our own private prayers. Note that there is first a concentration, not confused but silent, then a vocal prayer, then a giving of gratitude, and then waiting upon the Lord with our hearts sensitive, and speaking, or at least, in private life, knowing what comes by the Spirit. Did that happen, that aftermath? Yes. The Prophet says in his journal: "The quorum of the Seventy enjoyed a great flow of the Holy Spirit. Many arose and spoke, testifying that they were filled with the Holy Ghost, which was like fire in their bones, so that they could not hold their peace, but were constrained to cry hosanna to God and the Lamb, and glory in the highest." (Smith, *History of the Church,* 2:391–92.)

Of a similar occasion a few days before this one, Joseph said: "After these quorums were dismissed, I retired to my home, filled with the Spirit, and my soul cried hosanna to God and the Lamb, through the silent watches of the night; and while my eyes were closed in sleep, the visions of the Lord were sweet unto me, and His glory was round about me." (Smith, *History of the Church,* 2:387.) Much can be learned from that.

Half a century later, when forty years had passed since construction had begun on the Salt Lake Temple, the pattern the Prophet taught was used as Elder Lorenzo Snow led the Saints—some forty thousand of them—in the glorious privilege of uniting their voices in praise of the Lord that they had been able to reach the capstone. Forty thousand, and the shout was a shout! It echoed through the mountains. Can you imagine forty years of struggle and patience bursting out in joy as they did so! Well, that's acceptable to the Lord.

Another kind of shouting the Prophet rebuked. Let me in passing mention it. One time, Father Johnson asked a convert who had been a Methodist exhorter to pray in the family's evening worship. He hadn't overcome his habits. The exhorters in that old-time pattern were men who learned to throw their voice in a kind of falsetto quality. When the wind was right, they could be heard a mile away, some claim. This man began, literally, hallooing that way in prayer, and "alarmed the whole village." The Prophet was one of those who came running to the scene. In essence, he said, "Brother, don't pray like that again. You don't have to bray like a jackass to be heard of the Lord." (See Brigham Young, *Journal of Discourses,* 2:214.) Well, George A. Smith indicates that that brother left the Church. Now, if you're sincere, there's no problem. But there's something false and inconsistent about supposing that the Lord cannot hear you unless you halloo. He can hear the quietest turning of your own sacred conscience and knows the thoughts and intents of your heart.

The Prophet taught repeatedly that the Saints should be one in prayer, that when a group comes together in fasting and prayer, united in the petition of their hearts, that makes a greater difference somehow than if anyone alone had done so. The revelations say, "Be agreed as touching all things whatsoever ye ask of me." (D&C 27:18.) Be one in your prayers, for "if ye are not one ye are not mine." (D&C 38:27.) One of the sisters, the wife of George A. Smith, recalled the Prophet's statement to her. "He said that we did not know how to pray to have our prayers answered." But she added that when she and her husband received their endowments in the temple, they understood what he meant. (See Andrus and Andrus, *They Knew the Prophet,* 123.) The Lord instructed the Prophet to teach several of the brethren the keys whereby they might ask in prayer and receive an answer. (See D&C 124:95, 97.) Well, there is much about the privilege of the sanctuary that we cannot say outside the temple, but may I simply report that Brigham Young, who learned to pray listening to the Prophet, said repeatedly to the Saints that when someone prays in a congregation we should be saying in our minds what he or she is saying with the lips. We should repeat the very words in our minds, and then when we say amen we know what we're saying amen to. Without that repetition, sometimes we do not. Why is it important? So that the Saints may be one. Truly the effectual, fervent power of united prayer cannot be overestimated.

Later comment has to do with the original problem—the problem of guilt, the problem of sin. Here is the Prophet himself writing to his wife, saying, "I have called to mind all the past moments of my life and am left to mourn and shed tears of sorrow for my folly." (Larry E. Dahl and Donald Q. Cannon, *Encyclopedia of Joseph Smith's Teachings* [Salt Lake City:Bookcraft, 1997], 494.)

If we study them closely we find that all the Saints have had their struggles. Nephi, just to name one, writes with such strength in those first and early chapters that you wonder if he ever doubted or murmured or had a setback. The contrast between his attitude and even that of his own parents is startling. But in the fourth chapter of 2 Nephi, you will notice, he opens his soul and levels with us. And even though he has been struggling with the burden of leadership, he says, "When I desire to rejoice, my heart groaneth because of my sins." (v. 19.) Then he prays with a power that reminds one of David in the Psalms, "O Lord, wilt thou encircle me around in the robe of thy righteousness . . . make a way for mine escape." (v. 33.)

A homely illustration of the same point is the story about the two farmers talking, and there's a horse pulling the plow, but on his right flank, every time he pulls, the strap rubs what has become an open, gaping sore. The observer says, "Pretty tough on that horse to make him pull when he's got a gaping sore." The other farmer replies, "Yes, plumb tough, but I reckon we wouldn't get much work done in this world if we waited until everyone was plumb fit." And that's true in the Church. We wouldn't get any work done in the Church if we waited until all of us were perfect. The Lord wouldn't be able to call anyone to any position in the Church if he waited until we were all fully worthy.

If I may be personal for a moment, when I was called to be a mission president, the call was made by President Henry D. Moyle. I was taken aback by it, and surprised that he didn't ask any hard questions. I reminded him of that. "You haven't asked any questions of worthiness." He said, "Well, when one responds as you have, we don't have many questions." That didn't satisfy me. I said, "But President Moyle, I love the Church, but I have some problems." He came around the desk, put his arm around me, and said, "Brother Madsen, the Lord has to show a lot of mercy to let any of us work in His Church." That's true. But what does one do when he feels, as Lorenzo Snow put it, "that the heavens are as brass over his head." (See *Juvenile Instructor,* 22:22.) That though he ought to pray, he doesn't feel like praying. And when he does feel like praying, he is so ashamed that he hardly can. What then? My response is this glimpse from the Prophet.

The period just prior to the dedication of the Kirtland Temple saw an outpouring of the Spirit. Many of the brethren saw glorious visions, and the Prophet himself had a manifestation in which he saw, in panoramic vision, the lives of the Brethren of the Twelve— saw them in their strugglings, their flounderings, saw them preaching the gospel, saw them eventually brought back into the celestial kingdom. Interestingly, he saw them together—a group of them at least—as he recorded it, "in foreign lands." He didn't say England, but that's where they eventually went. He saw them, standing in a circle, beaten, tattered, their feet swollen, and clearly discouraged. Now, there are different levels of discouragement; we can be disturbed a bit, we can be worried, we can then be despondent, and there are moments in life for some of us when we ask, "What is the use?" And when we sink that far, we're almost to the point of wishing we could cease to be.

Well, the Prophet didn't indicate that it had gone that far with the Twelve, but they were looking down in their discouragement. Yet standing above them in the air was the Lord Jesus Christ. And it was made known to the Prophet that He yearned to show himself to them—to reach down and lift them—but they did not see Him. And the Savior looked upon them and wept. (See Smith, *History of the Church,* 2:381.) We're told by three of the Brethren who heard the Prophet rehearse that vision that he could never speak of it without himself weeping. Why? Why would he be so touched? Because he knew that Christ willingly came into the world and took upon himself the pains and sicknesses of His people so that He might be filled with compassion so that all the Father's family could come to Him, if to no one else—and sometimes there is no one else—could come to Him, knowing that He knows what is taking place in us when we sin, or suffer affliction, or are discouraged. The great tragedy of life is that, loving us and having paid that awful price of suffering, in the moment when He is now prepared to reach down and help us, we won't let Him. We look down instead of up, accepting the adversary's promptings that we must not pray; we cannot pray; we are not worthy to pray. But, says Nephi in response to that, "I say unto you that ye must pray always, and not faint." (2 Nephi 32:8–9.)

There may be things that we are unworthy to do at times in our life, but there is one thing we are never unworthy to do, and that is pray. I have a testimony about this. The Prophet Joseph Smith not only taught it, but exemplified it. You go to the Lord regardless of the condition of your soul, and He will respond. He never closes the door against you. You may close it against Him, but if so that is your initiative, not His. We should call upon Him when we need Him most, and that's usually when we feel least worthy, and then He can respond.

In the modern prophet Joseph Smith we have an example of living, breathing prayer—the kind that changes life. His early successes with prayer were the foundation of a pattern that brought him progressively closer to God. If prayer had no other function than to help us concentrate on the deepest concerns of our life— even to reveal ourselves to ourselves—it would be worth doing.

But beyond that the Prophet illustrates for all time that prayer isn't just subjective, it isn't just self-hypnosis. Rather, it is a plan and pattern whereby we do in fact break through the veil and receive at the living hand of the living God through His Christ.

Improving Communication with Our Heavenly Father

PRESIDENT EZRA TAFT BENSON

ALL THROUGH MY life the counsel to depend on prayer has been prized above almost any other advice I have ever received. It has become an integral part of me, an anchor, a constant source of strength, and the basis of my knowledge of things divine.

"Remember that whatever you do or wherever you are, you are never alone," was my father's familiar counsel. "Our Heavenly Father is always near. You can reach out and receive his aid through prayer." I have found this counsel to be true. Thank God we can reach out and tap that unseen power, without which no man can do his best.

The holy scriptures are replete with convincing admonitions regarding the importance of prayer, impressive examples of prayer, and counsel on how to pray effectively.

During his earthly ministry Jesus said, "Men ought always to pray, and not to faint." (Luke 18:1.) "Watch and pray," he said, "that ye enter not into temptation." (Matthew 26:41.) In this dispensation he said, "Pray always lest that wicked one have power in you, and remove you out of your place." (D&C 93:49.)

Through Joseph Smith the warning came, "And in nothing doth man offend God, or against none is his wrath kindled, save those who confess not his hand in all things, and obey not his commandments." (D&C 59:21.)

Then we have this instruction from our risen Lord as he ministered among the Nephite people on this Western Hemisphere:

"Ye must watch and pray always, lest ye be tempted by the devil, and ye be led away captive by him.

"Ye must watch and pray always lest ye enter into temptation; for Satan desireth to have you, that he may sift you as wheat.

"Therefore ye must always pray unto the Father in my name;

"And whatsoever ye shall ask the Father in my name, which is right, believing that ye shall receive, behold it shall be given unto you." (3 Nephi 18:15, 18–20.)

May I now suggest some ways to improve our communication with our Heavenly Father.

1. We should pray frequently. We should be alone with our Heavenly Father at least two or three times each day: "Morning, mid-day, and evening," as the scripture indicates. (Alma 34:21.) In addition, we are told to pray always. (2 Nephi 32:9; D&C 88:126.) This means that our hearts should be full, drawn out in prayer unto our Heavenly Father continually. (Alma 34:27.)

2. We should find an appropriate place where we can meditate and pray. We are admonished that this should be "in your closets, and your secret places, and in your wilderness." (Alma 34:26.) That is, it should be free from distraction, in secret. (3 Nephi 13:5–6.)

3. We should prepare ourselves for prayer. If we don't feel like praying, then we should pray until we do feel like praying. We should be humble. (D&C 112:10.) We should pray for forgiveness and mercy. (Alma 34:17–18.) We must forgive anyone against whom we have bad feelings. (Mark 11:25.) Yet, the scriptures warn, our prayers will be vain if we "turn away the needy, and the naked, and visit not the sick and afflicted, and impart [not] of [our] substance." (Alma 34:28.)

4. Our prayers should be meaningful and pertinent. We should not use the same phrases at each prayer. Each of us would become disturbed if a friend said the same few words to us each day, treated the conversation as a chore, and could hardly wait to finish in order to turn on the TV and forget us.

In all of our prayers it is well to use the sacred pronouns of the scriptures—*thee, thou, thy,* and *thine* when addressing Deity in prayer, instead of the more common pronouns *you, your,* and *yours.* In this arrangement we show greater respect to Deity.

For what should we pray? We should pray about our work, against the power of our enemies and the devil, for our welfare and the welfare of those around us. (Alma 34:20, 22, 25, 27.) We should counsel with the Lord pertaining to all our decisions and activities. (Alma 37:36–37.) We should be grateful enough to give thanks for all we have. We should confess his hand in all things. (D&C 59:21.) Ingratitude is one of our great sins.

The Lord has declared in modern revelation: "And he who receiveth all things with thankfulness shall be made glorious; and the things of this earth shall be added unto him, even an hundred fold, yea, more." (D&C 78:19.)

We should ask for what we need, taking care that we not ask for things that would be to our detriment. (James 4:3.) We should ask for strength to overcome our problems. (Alma 31:31–33.) We should pray for the inspiration and well-being of the President of the Church, the General Authorities, our stake president, our bishop, our quorum president, our home teachers, our family members, and our civic leaders. Many other suggestions could be made, but with the help of the Holy Ghost, we will know about what we should pray. (Romans 8:26.)

5. After making a request through prayer, we have a responsibility to assist in its being granted. We should listen. Perhaps while we are on our knees, the Lord wants to counsel us. "Sincere praying implies that when we ask for any virtue or blessing, we should work for the blessing and cultivate the virtue." (David O. McKay, *True to the Faith* [Salt Lake City: Bookcraft, 1966], 208.)

When I was a young missionary in northern England in 1922, opposition to the Church became very intense. The opposition became so strong that the mission president asked that we discontinue all street meetings, and in some places tracting was also discontinued.

My companion and I had been invited to travel over to South Shields and speak in sacrament meeting. In the invitation we were told, "We feel sure we can fill the little chapel. Many of the people over here do not believe the falsehoods printed about us. If you'll come, we're sure that we'll have a great meeting." We accepted.

We fasted and prayed sincerely and went to the sacrament meeting. My companion had planned to talk on the first principles of the gospel. I had studied hard in preparation for a talk on the apostasy. There was a wonderful spirit in the meeting. My companion spoke first and gave an inspirational message. I responded and talked with a freedom I had never experienced before in my life. When I sat down, I realized that I had not mentioned the apostasy. I had talked on the Prophet Joseph Smith and borne my witness of his divine mission and the truthfulness of the Book of Mormon.

After the meeting ended, many people came forward, including several nonmembers, and said, "Tonight we received a witness that Mormonism is true. We are now ready for baptism."

This was an answer to our fasting and prayers, for we prayed to say only those things which would touch the hearts of the investigators.

In 1946 I was assigned by President George Albert Smith to go to war-torn Europe to reestablish our missions from Norway to South Africa, and to set up a program for the distribution of welfare supplies—food, clothing, bedding, etc.

We established headquarters in London. We then made preliminary arrangements with the military on the continent. One of the first men I wished to see was the commander of the American forces in Europe. He was stationed in Frankfurt, Germany.

When we arrived in Frankfurt, my companion and I went in to seek an appointment with the general. The appointment officer said, "Gentlemen, there will be no opportunity for you to see the general for at least three days. He's very busy and is filled up with appointments." I said, "It is very important that we see him and we can't wait that long. We're due in Berlin tomorrow." He said, "I'm sorry."

We left the building, went out to our car, removed our hats, and united in prayer. We then went back into the building and found a different officer at the appointment post. In less than fifteen minutes we were in the presence of the general. We had prayed that we would be able to see him and to touch his heart, knowing that all relief supplies contributed from any source were required to be placed into the hands of the military for distribution.

Our objective, as we explained it to the general, was to distribute our own supplies to our own people, through our own channels, and also to make gifts for general child feeding. We explained the welfare program and how it operated. Finally, he said, "Well, gentlemen, you go ahead and collect your supplies, and by the time you get them collected, the policy may be changed." We said, "General, our supplies are already collected, they're always collected. Within twenty-four hours from the time I wire the First Presidency of the Church in Salt Lake City, carloads of supplies will be rolling toward Germany. We have many storehouses filled with basic commodities." He then said, "I've never heard of a people with such vision." His heart was touched as we had prayed it would be. Before we left his office we had a written authorization to make our own distribution to our own people through our own channels.

It is soul-satisfying to know that God is mindful of us and ready to respond when we place our trust in him and do that which is right. There is no place for fear among men and women who place their trust in the Almighty, who do not hesitate to humble themselves in seeking divine guidance through prayer. Though persecutions arise, though reverses come, in prayer we can find reassurance, for God will speak peace to the soul. That peace, that spirit of serenity, is life's greatest blessing.

As a boy in the Aaronic Priesthood, I learned this little poem about prayer. It has remained with me.

> *I know not by what methods rare,*
> *But this I know: God answers prayer.*
> *I know that He has given His word,*
> *Which tells me prayer is always heard,*
> *And will be answered soon or late,*
> *And so I pray and calmly wait.*
> *I know not if the message sought*
> *Will come just in the way I thought;*
> *But leave my prayers with Him alone*

Whose ways are wiser than my own,
Assured that He will grant my quest,
Or send some answer far more blessed.

I bear witness that God lives. He is not dead. I bear testimony that God, our Father, with his Beloved Son, our Savior, did in very deed appear to Joseph Smith. I know this as I know that I live.

I testify that there is a God in heaven who hears and answers prayer. I know this to be true, for he has answered mine. I would humbly urge all persons—member and nonmember alike—to keep in close touch with our Father in heaven through prayer. Never before in this gospel dispensation has there been a greater need for prayer. That we will constantly depend upon our Heavenly Father and conscientiously strive to improve our communication with him is my earnest plea.

Preparation
for Prayer

ELDER MARION D. HANKS

UNDER DIVINE law the blessings of prayer, like salvation, are enjoyed by each individual in that measure which we are "willing to receive" (D&C 88:32), rather than in any inscrutable outpouring or withholding from the heavens. Our loving Father in heaven desires our eternal joy, knows that such joy accompanies true Christlike character which can only be developed through the proper exercise of our free agency, and so has made available to us the rules for eternal happiness, with his Spirit to guide us; provided a circumstance in which there is "opposition in all things"; and "given unto man that he should act for himself."

Under these principles, we limit what God can do for us by our willful ignorance or disobedience or selfishness or lack of faith. Speaking of those who will not qualify for any of the kingdoms of his glory but accept instead a "kingdom not of glory," he has said through a prophet:

"They shall return again to their own place, to enjoy that which they are willing to receive, because they were not willing to enjoy that which they might have received.

"For what doth it profit a man if a gift is bestowed upon him, and he receive not the gift? Behold, he rejoices not in that which is given unto him, neither rejoices in him who is the giver of the gift." (D&C 88:32–33.)

This principle applies also to prayer. We will enjoy the blessings we are willing to receive.

The scriptures repeatedly admonish and invite us to pray, but some of us have never accepted the invitation. Others make occasional attempts at prayer but feel unrewarded, the petition seemingly unheeded. For many, prayer may be largely formula or habit. Perhaps the kind of prayer most widely, if infrequently, experienced has been the pleas of anguish, imploring heavenly intervention in present or pending calamity, or in the aborting of the consequences of some foolish act or unwise decision.

But there are also those who have a rich prayer experience, a prayer life, a consistent, rewarding relationship with the Lord in a real and responsive way. How is that blessing brought about? How can we develop that kind of prayer relationship?

Consider these different experiences with prayer and the results of each, and where we individually may be in the program.

1. It is certain that if we do not pray, we do not receive the blessings of prayer. Like one who has never really enjoyed a great poem or a good book, a painting or a symphony or a sunset, we may live on unaware, missing, perhaps even disdaining, what we will not enjoy. Instead, we experience that which we are willing to receive.

2. Deep need or personal crises motivate some of the most earnest prayers we ever offer. Sin, fear, anxiety, an unsupportable

burden—these drive us, rather than beckon us, to prayer. When we are pressed by great affliction or threatened in our personal life, when tribulation is upon us, we turn to God. All who are acquainted with prayer and who have lived long enough to experience life's complexities and vicissitudes understand this kind of reaching for the Lord. We know what it is to cry out to God in sorrowing penitence or deep necessity, or perhaps in great gratitude. The spontaneity of these outcryings—these "groanings" of the soul—is normal and natural and issues from a relationship with our Heavenly Father that is intuitively felt, whether or not nurtured or ever acknowledged to self in comfortable seasons. Such occasions are usually not premeditated or pre-thought or prepared; they issue from our depths, from anguish or despair or shame or humble gratitude, often with tears, and they signify the reality of that which in every human is more than human, something that identifies us with a power and spirit far loftier and lovelier than our own, with a caring Father with whom we have part as his beloved children.

But such special times of anxiety or fear or exultation of spirit, sincere and important as they are, are like occasional calls home when our more thoughtful and regular attendance would be welcome, and is expected.

3. Less availing, perhaps, are the sporadic efforts that occur when we think we are too tired or too busy, but are nudged into motion by the remembrance of other times and other circumstances when our faith was more simple or our needs more pressing, and we were not too tired or too busy to pray more consistently and confidently. We pray because we know we ought to pray, and we are responsive enough to take a minute to go through the motions.

4. But suppose we *are* reporting with regularity, but do it merely as a matter of habit, our thoughts elsewhere, our minds

inattentive to the communication, our hearts not in it, our words the language learned long ago from others and never changed or challenged through personal needs or matured spiritual strength. Some of us pray like that. We say our prayers by rote, as ritual, missing much of the meaning and purpose of prayer and therefore its value. Not really believing, perhaps not really even paying attention, we may be repeating little phrases from childhood signifying nothing, words without worship, form without feeling, prayer that scarcely leaves our lips, involving neither emotions nor mind nor spirit.

We can and should do better. We can open channels of consolation and courage, and consolidate the powers in our own personality. We can set in motion and put into focus forces we have only heard about or dimly dreamed of and never had faith enough to seek for or really believe in or expect to have functioning in our own behalf.

Twice in recent years accounts have appeared in newspapers of communities suffering from insufficient water supplies and pressure, who have undertaken costly studies and planned extensive improvements only to discover by chance that the main valve of the water system in the towns was only partially open. They had been surviving on a thin stream and weak force when they could have at any time enjoyed vastly enhanced power simply by turning on the valve.

Prayer is like that.

Deep wellsprings of living water are available and accessible to us, a limitless source of spiritual sustenance, of guidance and comfort and divine love.

We can open up the line. That is what preparation for prayer can help us accomplish.

We are not talking about making prayer more difficult, or

necessarily longer, or surrounding it with formalities, or making it seem mysterious. Prayer is the simple act of communicating with God; it is an act of worship and usually involves talking and listening. The unspoken "yearnings of our hearts" or the "groanings of the spirit" also go up to God, it is sure. We should pray when we feel like praying, and we should also pray when we do not much feel like praying, and the formalities are obviously of little concern to him. The important thing is to reach out for him in faith and love. But our prayers can mean much more to us and be more effective in bringing about God's purposes for us if we are prepared for the experience in the way he has directed.

The ancient prophet Samuel, speaking to all the house of Israel, said: "Prepare your hearts unto the Lord, and serve him only." (1 Samuel 7:3.)

God's stalwart servant Job, suffering the agonies of his deprivation and pain, was told, "Prepare thine heart, and stretch out thine hands toward him." (Job 11:13.)

We are taught that God, who knows our hearts and our needs before we ever come to him, will help us prepare ourselves and in effect speak through us as we pray to him. "The preparations of the heart in man, and the answer of the tongue, is from the Lord." (Proverbs 16:1.)

If the question should be asked, "What sense is there in prayer if God already knows our needs and in effect is speaking through us to himself," then the answer is the same answer that applies to all that he expects of us: He wants us to be involved, to have the experience, to make the effort, knowing that only in this way do we really understand, commit our hearts, and grow.

There are many classic cases of preparation preceding prayer. Consider several of these.

1. Enos. In his youth Enos had been taught in "the nurture and admonition of the Lord," and the teachings of his father had "sunk deep" into his heart. As he was hunting in the forest one day, the thoughts he had often heard his father speak "concerning eternal life, and the joy of the saints" came to him with such force that his "soul hungered"; and he "kneeled down before [his] maker and . . . cried unto him in mighty prayer and supplication for [his] own soul." (Enos 1:1, 3–4.)

Instruction faithfully and patiently given, quiet contemplation, and that great moment of need when his "soul hungered" combined to bring about a condition in which Enos's prayers to God engendered the most meaningful experience of his life. The marvelous consequences are taught in one short, very significant chapter as the book of Enos in the Book of Mormon.

2. Nephi. The record teaches us that Nephi, being very young and "having great desires to know of the mysteries of God, . . . did cry unto the Lord; and behold he did visit me, and did soften my heart that I did believe all the words which had been spoken by my father." (1 Nephi 2:16.) A boy, patiently and lovingly taught by a good father, early enjoyed the great desire to know for himself, and in the intensity of that desire went to the Lord and received his answer.

3. Oliver Cowdery. Oliver Cowdery was promised a knowledge of the Book of Mormon records if he would "ask in faith, with an honest heart, believing." The promise was unequivocal. He would know in his mind and heart by the Holy Ghost, through the spirit of revelation. He was invited to ask that he might know the mysteries of God and that he might "translate and receive knowledge from all those ancient records which have been hid up, that are sacred," with the promise that "according to your faith shall it be done unto you." (D&C 8:1, 11.)

Oliver tried to translate but did not succeed, and he was told that he had "not understood" but had supposed God would give it to him "when you took no thought save it was to ask me.

"But, behold, I say unto you, that you must study it out in your mind; *then* you must ask me if it be right, and if it is right I will cause that your bosom shall burn within you; therefore, you shall feel that it is right.

"But if it be not right, you shall have no such feelings, but you shall have a stupor of thought that shall cause you to forget the thing which is wrong." (D&C 9:7–9; emphasis added.)

4. Moroni. Moroni exhorted the Lamanites that when they should receive the translated record of the Book of Mormon and should "read these things," they should remember the Lord's mercy unto his children from the creation of Adam to the present, and "ponder it" in their hearts. Thus having received, read, meditated, and been grateful, and pondered these things in their hearts, then they were to "ask God, the Eternal Father, in the name of Christ, if these things are not true." If they should ask "with a sincere heart, with real intent, having faith in Christ," God would manifest the truth unto them by the power of the Holy Ghost. (Moroni 10:3–5.)

In all these accounts there is one consistent message: Preparation for prayer can help communication with the Lord become an experience full of meaning and full of love, and can help to bring about the realization of God's purposes, and of our appropriate purposes, in prayer.

Our *hearts* must be prepared for prayer, for the instruction is that we are to go to him with "all our hearts," with lowliness of heart, with sincerity of heart, with honest hearts, and with broken and contrite hearts.

If our hearts are really right and committed to the Lord, we will go to him with confidence, with, as the psalmist said, "expectation" in the Lord (Psalm 62:5), believing that we shall receive. The fullness of our blessings and the soul-satisfying answers to our prayers will come when we learn to "yield our hearts" unto the Lord:

"Nevertheless they did fast and pray oft, and did wax stronger and stronger in their humility, and firmer and firmer in the faith of Christ, unto the filling their souls with joy and consolation, yea, even to the purifying and the sanctification of their hearts, which sanctification cometh because of their yielding their hearts unto God." (Helaman 3:35.)

God expects us to come to him with our spirits in tune, ready to yield our hearts unto him. If we will do this, we have his promise, and we will receive the blessings.

Our *minds* also need to be prepared for prayer. Through search and study we can begin to learn what we need to know. And we must think—actively, consciously, quietly, reflectively, honestly, deeply think. Then we can in good conscience come to the Lord to seek wisdom, comfort, strength, grace, or courage. When we know our own needs, know what we have to be thankful for, know what our responsibility is to God and others, then, with our souls hungry and our desires strong and honest, we can approach the Lord with earnest questions, appropriate petitions, and grateful minds.

As our minds and hearts are prepared, so must our *spirits* be subdued and sensitive if we desire to drink deeply from the spring. We are to go to him in confidence, believing that we shall receive. John assures us: "And this is the confidence that we have in him, that, if we ask any thing according to his will, he heareth us: And if we know that he hear us, whatsoever we ask, we know that we have the petitions that we desired of him." (1 John 5:14–15.)

There is another form of preparation for prayer that must be considered, and that is the *condition of our lives* as a testimony of our determination and effort to obey his commandments. One of the most beautiful promises given by the Lord to Joseph Smith was that "if ye are purified and cleansed from all sin, ye shall ask whatsoever you will in the name of Jesus and it shall be done." (D&C 50:29.)

Consistently the scriptures teach that the Lord expects us to approach him with clean hands, having prepared ourselves for the visit. We are to repent and forsake sins, turn away from evil, learn to keep his commandments and to abide in him as his word abides in us.

Our relationships with others must be right. Before we take our gift to the altar, we are to correct matters that separate us from our neighbors. The admonition is to forgive others and to confess our faults and pray for one another as we ask for forgiveness for ourselves. King Benjamin taught his people that they were to believe in God and in his almighty power, to recognize their own limitations, to repent of their sins and forsake them, and to humble themselves before God and ask in sincerity of heart for his forgiveness. (Mosiah 4:9–10.)

The records are clear and understandable. We are to be prayerful and thankful in our hearts always, to seek his presence regularly, and to talk over with him all the matters that concern us, large and small. We are to go to him in times of penitence and in times of gratitude; when we need wisdom, when our souls hunger, when we have need to commune with him. Yet he expects us to come with our minds and hearts right and our spirits in tune, ready to yield our hearts unto him.

In our personal lives, then, and in our homes and families, how shall we prepare for prayer? In all the ways mentioned, with these specific suggestions:

Read the scriptures. When Nephi wrote the story of his father's experience with the Lord, he talked of Lehi's vision in which a person descended out of the midst of heaven and gave Lehi a book and "bade him that he should read. And . . . as he read, he was filled with the Spirit of the Lord." (1 Nephi 1:11–12.)

So may we, as we read the scriptures, receive the Spirit of the Lord. The stories from scripture mentioned above, and countless others, will help us get the spirit of prayer. The sacred records speak knowledge and understanding to us, lead to testimony, and offer ways of application to us individually; they will help us to want to pray and lead us to experience prayer.

Fast. This is a wonderful way to prepare ourselves for prayer. Fasting and prayer go together. The subduing of the spirit by the discipline of the appetites is a divinely directed avenue to accomplishing the purposes of prayer.

Meditate. We need to actively, consciously think about the Lord and our relationship with him, about his goodness to us and our forebears, about the gratitude we should feel for all he has given and does now give us. To quietly consider and reflect upon our blessings is an exercise of high value and great benefit.

Discuss these matters with our families before family prayer. We should be calling to the attention of our children and their children the special kindnesses and graciousness of the Lord to us through his gifts, especially the gift of his Holy Son and all that he means to us.

It will bless all of us to think about and speak of our covenants made solemnly in sacred places and renewed regularly through partaking the sacrament. We can share feelings and impressions and experiences with those nearest and dearest to us. This done before prayer will bring tender and humbling sentiments and spiritual emotions to our hearts.

A quiet moment of conversation about our experiences with

ourselves, with our families, with others, and with the Lord can be fruitful. What were the good things we did today? What were the actions and language and relationships that were not good? What was the genealogy of our behavior, good or bad, today? What were its roots, and how can they be traced to earlier thoughts or behavior? to attitudes we perhaps need to examine? How can we improve?

There are other ways of preparation for prayer. Contemplation of the beauty of God's wonderful world, communing with nature in lovely places, experiencing the uplift of great music or great literature—these and other ways bring us enhanced capacity and encourage us, strengthen us, and help us in an attitude of thankfulness and prayerfulness.

In the three essential relationships of life—with ourselves, with others, and with God—there must be unity and wholeness if we are to be happy. Whenever we, through inspiration and determination, through penitence and reconciliation, bring about greater integrity in any of these relationships, we can appropriately approach the Lord seeking his sanctifying Spirit to give divine stamp of approval to our honest efforts. We may come to him in prayer with the certainty that we are heard and that he will help. In our burdens and anxiety and times of moral weakness we have of ourselves no strength sufficient for the need. Why not try God? He is our ready source of power. He wants to help us, and he will help us, according to his great wisdom and his great love and his knowledge of our needs. Of this I personally know, as I know that preparation for praying makes prayer a sweeter and lovelier and more meaningful experience.

May each of us be transformed by the renewing of our minds, and know that which is "good, and acceptable, and perfect" in the Lord.

Pray with All Energy of Heart

Ann N. Madsen

I MET FOURTEEN-year-old Julie Wang several decades ago in K'Liau, Taiwan. She was a new convert to the Church. We corresponded, and later she came to visit America and stayed with us. I asked her to teach my Mia Maid class about prayer. She said shyly, "What can I teach them?" I said, "Just tell them how you pray." So she did. "I pray like this," she said. "I say, 'Hello, God, this is Julie Wang,' then I wait, and he says, 'Hello, Julie.'" My class and I were taken off guard by her simple faith in a God who is alive, listening, and ready to respond. She taught all of us that day. One thing I have learned is that there are as many ways to pray as there are people. The one prerequisite is that we "pray . . . with all . . . energy of heart." (Moroni 7:48.)

How does prayer work? I don't presume to offer you a paradigm, a perfect pattern for everyone. Instead, I want to examine my own prayer life, beginning with my earliest memory of my sweet father saying in our family prayers, "We come to thee on the bended knees of our body, Father." How humble that made me feel.

Today, I love to pray. Ask my husband. I'm always poking him and saying, "Shouldn't we pray now?" But I didn't always. Nine milestones in my own prayer history will illustrate how this process unfolded in me. I hope these will bring similar moments to your mind.

1. Under the old-fashioned, six-foot-high rose bush, which was like a cave to an eight-year-old, I made my first attempt the week after my baptism at praying for repentance. I had lied about practicing the piano. I'd messed up my music books to look like I had practiced, but I'd put in only half the time I'd claimed. Prior to my baptism, my father had done a good job of explaining personal responsibility to me. He almost scared me to death, I think, and I'm so grateful. In that solitary confinement of my rose bush, I knew enough to cry a bit, say how sorry I was, and ask for help not to tell lies ever again. I soon found that I sometimes *did* do it again and that the best of intentions wavered when friends called me to come out to play. I learned to repent until I got it right.

I've continued to learn in the sixty-plus years since my baptism. I have learned to say "I'm sorry" when I pray, to take my shame humbly before the Lord, to take responsibility for my actions. During the sacrament is an especially meaningful time to do this. I'm learning to forgive—everybody, everything, every time—because I truly want to be forgiven. I'm also learning to pray to love those more whom I have loved less. I understand why God requires this of us. He loves us all more. He wants us to be like him. I understand all this much better than I did that first time as a newly baptized member weeping under a sheltering rose bush.

2. Even saying the word *Brighton* stirs deep feelings in me. I was

thirteen years old and just finishing an idyllic week at the Brighton MIA Girls' Home in Big Cottonwood Canyon. It was Sunday, and sitting in tall meadow grasses on a mountainside strewn with white granite boulders on a sunny, summer day, we had listened to an inspired Sunday School teacher bear witness to us. Then all of us knelt together in the tall grass, almost invisible to any passerby, while a young man about to serve a mission prayed in a way I had never heard before—he addressed God directly—and suddenly I didn't dare open my eyes because I knew for certain that God was a person and I felt him unmistakably near. At that moment and ever since, I have known that God is a living, loving, powerful being. After the others had wandered back down the trail, my best friend and I knelt once more, hidden under an overhanging pine bough. We didn't say much to each other, but we each knelt down and poured out our hearts in gratitude. We both knew what had happened and felt a tremendous need to tell the Lord how grateful we were that we'd come to know him.

I have learned since then that kneeling and speaking aloud to our Father in a quiet place daily gives focus to my faith. I have a window in my walk-in closet, and I pray there at dawn, each morning. I enter my closet and shut the door, exactly as the scriptures direct. I feel really good just to have done that much right each day.

We can pray any place, any time—beside a mountain trail at Brighton, kneeling in a closet, anywhere. We are the ones who choose the when and the where. No time is wrong. The only prerequisite is a broken heart and a contrite spirit. And I think *broken* can mean more than the painful process we think of in repentance. *Broken* can also mean open, not hardened and inaccessible but open and ready to receive, to make place for the Lord's direction. The scriptures teach us to "pray *always,* and I will pour out my Spirit upon you, and great shall be your blessing." (D&C 19:38; emphasis added.) Does this mean keeping up a running conversation with the Lord every waking hour? Yes! He has taught, "Look unto me in *every* thought; doubt not, fear not." (D&C 6:36; emphasis added.) So be informal; be formal; be all ways prayerful. Formal, kneeling prayers help us focus and cut out distractions. Consider locking the door, turning off the phone, savoring the silence. Perhaps setting your alarm for ten to fifteen minutes earlier than usual would enable you to enjoy the quiet before the three-year-old gets up or the baby cries. When we reverently enter the presence of the Lord in prayer, we can feel like guests in heaven.

3. A few months after my mountaintop experience at Brighton, well after midnight one night, I finished reading the Book of Mormon for the first time. I had been reading it in my closet, because my dad had told me to turn off the light. (I was devious then, I confess.) I had excitedly finished, anxious to put Moroni's promise to the test. My dear teacher and friend, Oscar Hunter, week after week, pleaded with a group of youth attending his weekly ward fireside not to take his word only but to find out for ourselves. He urged us to read the Book of Mormon and do exactly what Moroni invites. At last, I could ask that prayer, because I had finished the book from cover to cover—except those tedious chunks of Isaiah, which I didn't understand. (This makes my students, children, and husband smile because I now teach Isaiah classes at BYU.)

As I knelt beside my bed, I was excited, full of faith, and prepared to entertain an angel should my answer come by that means. I used Moroni's words exactly: "I am asking with a sincere heart, with real intent, having faith in Christ, if this book is not true." (I remember wondering why it said "is not true." Why don't I ask if it "is true"? But the scriptures said "is not true," and I didn't dare say any other words because I wanted Moroni's promise to be answered.) In the guileless innocence of youth I repeated that plea over and over. I resolved I would not get up from my knees until I had my answer. After what seemed a very long time, it came. In an unmistakable way I felt the Spirit from my head to my toes, filling me with a warmth I could not deny. I remember a heartfelt thank-you as I jumped to my feet, rushed to my window, and barely restrained myself from shouting to all the world, "It's true! Joseph Smith is a prophet!" Thus began a lifelong study that continues to this moment. I can never get enough of the gospel of Jesus Christ. I learned for myself about the Holy Ghost and the reality of the Restoration—and I learned that God truly answers prayers.

Since that singular day, I have learned to ask for the daily guidance of the Holy Ghost. I have experienced what Isaiah describes when he says, "Thine ears shall hear a word behind thee, saying, This is the way, walk ye in it." (Isaiah 30:21.) The Holy Ghost guides us into the will of God and away from temptation. He speaks directly to my spirit. Sometimes, when I have made up my mind, he causes me to question my confidence. At other, less-certain times, when I am confused or discouraged, I have learned to ask what I should pray for—ask in a prayer what to say in a prayer. As I learned from Paul's writing to the Romans: "Likewise the Spirit also helpeth our infirmities: for we know not what we should pray for as we ought: but the Spirit itself maketh intercession for us with *sighings* which cannot be uttered." (Romans 8:26.) (I chose to use the alternate translation from the Greek here: *sighings* instead of *groanings*. See Romans 8:26, footnote d, in the LDS edition of the King James Version of the Bible.)

Joseph Smith made significant changes in that verse. "The Spirit maketh intercession for us with *striving* which cannot be *expressed*." (Joseph Smith, *Teachings of the Prophet Joseph Smith,* sel.

Joseph Fielding Smith [Salt Lake City: Deseret Book, 1970], 278; emphasis added.)

So the Holy Ghost translates and delivers our pleadings and praises to our Father even when we can't find the words to express our deepest joy or darkest sorrow. When you can't find words, trust the Spirit. Modern revelation teaches us: "He that asketh in Spirit shall receive in Spirit. . . . He that asketh in the Spirit asketh according to the will of God; wherefore it is done even as he asketh." (D&C 46:28, 30.)

4. In the following years, my testimony grew, as I listened intently in seminary and then ate up every word offered me at the University of Utah institute of religion. The summer after high school I met and fell in love with a handsome young man—who was not a Latter-day Saint. We began reading the Book of Mormon together, and I was sure he would join the Church. In the middle of this process, he begged me to marry him. I thought I would—one year to the day after he was baptized, when we could go to the temple. My prayers began to move from, "I know how great my joy will be with this one soul I'm bringing to you" to "Father, should I marry Bob?"

I was a freshman at the University of Utah, working part-time at ZCMI during the Christmas break. Almost the moment I began asking the second prayer, "Is Bob the man I should marry?" a series of experiences and thoughts cumulatively answered me a resounding "No"! I remember the day the thought came, "Weren't you going to marry a returned missionary?" and I wondered when I had lost sight of that goal. Probably in the moonlight at Zion National Park, where we had worked the summer before. Day after day a former goal or idea surfaced in my mind. It was as if the Lord were saying to me gently but firmly, "What is it you don't understand about 'no'?" Finally, after about eight days of asking, I owned the answer to my prayer and told Bob no. I had learned that God could communicate clearly to me on important matters and could say no.

Since that painful day when I said no, even though I was sorely tempted to say yes, I have learned to pray to recognize temptations, no matter how subtle, and for the strength to flee from sin once recognized and to avoid going counter to God's will for me. Marrying Bob would have been going against God's will, which I was tempted to do. Temptation itself is not sin. In fact, as Elder Rulon G. Craven points out, temptation serves a purpose: we learn who we truly are when we are tempted; our strengths and weaknesses become brightly apparent to us as we respond to each temptation. (Rulon G. Craven, "Temptation," *Ensign,* May 1996, 77.) It's hard, but it's true. Life is truly a test. I have learned to pray for the strength to meet challenges, not to have them removed.

"Resist the devil, and he will flee from you" (James 4:7) is our sure promise. I teach that to my New Testament students, to my Isaiah students, to my Old Testament Roots students. In every class I teach, some time during the semester I tell them the great secret: "Resist the devil, and he will flee from you."

How grateful I am that Jesus taught us to meet temptation by paying no heed to it. I know we can lose all desire for sin. One day we will simply ignore the devil, not interested in the least in what he offers because we are so mightily interested in the promises of our Father to share all he has with us. So, I don't just pray not to be led into temptation, I pray to be led into understanding God's will for me. The basic purpose of prayer may well be to find out the will of God and then to ask for faith and strength to carry it out.

5. I told my granddaughter the other day that from the moment I broke off that "first love" relationship, I prayed about every boy I dated. It was tedious. "Is this the man I am going to marry?"—and

I would supply the name of my latest date. That is when I learned to continue in prayer, using "vain" repetition. I learned a modicum of patience but got tired of repeating those same words over and over again, filling in the blank. But one night, standing with Truman Madsen on a northern hillside overlooking the Salt Lake Valley, which was a jewel box of lights, I heard the whispered voice of the Spirit, "This is the man you're going to marry"—and I didn't believe it. I remember shaking my head and scolding myself for entertaining such a notion, but then it came again with more force. And yet again. And I learned how the Holy Ghost speaks with us, Spirit to spirit, putting words not our own into our minds in the customized, unmistakable way only he can communicate to each of us individually. I learned one way God can say *yes.* That was one of the most pivotal *yeses* I was ever able to recognize.

How do we know when our prayers are being answered? Sometimes we don't. Sometimes we don't want to, like investigators who put off praying to know if the Church is true because they are not ready to shoulder the responsibility of knowing.

I am continuing to learn how to recognize answers that come in unexpected ways. Sometimes he tells us directly "in our minds and in our hearts" (D&C 8:2), in words, like my answer on that breezy hilltop overlooking the Salt Lake Valley. I am learning to sort out his impressions from my own ideas. Sometimes I have a lot of great ideas. I want to do a lot of good things, and sometimes I can't tell whether it's really the Lord that wants me to do it or whether it's only my wanting to do it. It's one of the biggest problems I have. From Isaiah I've learned that the Lord's thoughts are not my thoughts—they are higher. "Neither are your ways my ways"—his are higher. (Isaiah 55:8–9.) That's how I can tell the difference. Sometimes a three-year-old's scripture, spoken confidently by heart on a Primary program, matches precisely my need. At times the opening hymn may tell me all he wishes to communicate to me, or the closing hymn, or the sacrament hymn. I bear you my witness that has been true for me. Often the gentle words of a friend, even the friends in my own home—my husband, my children, my grandchildren—hold the answer. And, don't forget, God has been giving answers for a long, long time and commanded those who received them to take notes. Search the scriptures. Your answer might be waiting for you there.

6. I began praying for children before Truman and I were even married, and from the moment we were married, we both prayed earnestly to begin our family. Truman was beginning his four-year Ph.D. work at Harvard. It never occurred to us to postpone our family. Kneeling at that altar in the Salt Lake Temple, we felt more than ready to welcome children into our home. (That's how young and ignorant we were—who is ever fully ready for children?) For nine months our pleading for children seemed to produce nothing, and I feared I would never have a child. Then I was pregnant! Five years later when Truman was a bishop and we had three children under four, I was frenzied but fulfilled. We were a year into Truman's teaching career at Brigham Young University. I went to my obstetrician at this point, anticipating that he would tell me that I was expecting our fourth child. (Our third was about seven months old at this time.) Instead, he told me I was not pregnant but had a problem.

During the next few years I had tests and surgery to enable me to bear more children. But the fear I had early in my marriage of not being able to bear children was now a reality. We prayed, pleading with the Lord to enable us to have more children. Then we were called to New England, where Truman would be a thirty-five-year-old mission president and I would be a twenty-nine-year-old "mission mother" and our three children under seven would live for the next three years in a wonderful old mission home. This, of course, was an amazing moment in our little family's life. When my doctor heard we would be in Boston, he was elated: the world-renowned Dr. John Rock had established the Rock Infertility Clinic there. I felt confident that this was to be the answer to our prayers.

After a thorough course of treatment, Dr. Rock gave me the medical verdict. I had evidently gone through a very early menopause and would have no more children. I was devastated. President Hugh B. Brown was touring our mission, and I asked him for a blessing. If the best of medical science couldn't do it, I was sure the Lord could handle it and, after all, I was serving him on a mission right now. It was only logical. Right? *Wrong.* In his eloquent blessing President Brown told me to "trouble the Lord no more on this matter." After I had cried my heart out, I asked President Brown what that meant, and he explained very simply that in my prayers I should no longer beg for a child. I learned about another kind of no. I learned to obey, to endure something that was totally against my will. I was *beginning* to learn "thy will, *not mine,* be done." That day I stopped praying for a baby.

7. During the years when our children were growing up, I performed a small ritual as I lay in bed after family prayer. I would put the name of each child before the Lord so that I could analyze the unique challenges he or she faced. Then I would ask for the Lord's help in being his instrument to nurture and guide. It was such a tender task. I looked forward to it and to the mornings that followed when many of my queries were answered quietly during that clean-slate time of just-after-awakening.

One of my great concerns during those late-night reveries was how to teach each of our children to really pray—to open conduits to their Heavenly Father. I remember thinking that this would be the best insurance we could leave them if anything should happen to us before they were grown. And so I prayed that they would learn that God hears and answers prayers.

About this time, during a severe drought, when the Wasatch Mountains had never greened through spring and summer, President Spencer W. Kimball asked us as a church to fast for rain on an appointed day. Our family did. During family home evening, we heard the rain begin to fall on the metal roof of our patio. It was an electric moment. At first it was just a few drops, but soon it was a torrent. We all ran outside, and one of our children said, "Let's kneel down here with the rain falling on us to thank the Lord." Then we all put around small bottles to catch the water. I've kept mine since that day; it's full of "holy" water. Our children learned part of the lesson then; God indeed hears and answers prayers. Their dripping faces and soaking clothes and water bottles clutched in their damp hands were tangible proof.

In addition, they learned that uniting our prayers with others changes the equation. Later, temple experiences taught them of a united upward reach, made more effective by kind feelings, full of love. Unity is powerful in prayer. Personal prayers reflected in family prayers make us one in purpose. I love to hear my husband use the exact words in our morning prayer that I have uttered in solitude just moments earlier in my own personal prayer. It is a wonderful coming together. To paraphrase a statement we all know, "If ye are one, ye are mine."

During the years since my first halting prayers, I have uttered many kinds of prayers. "Telegraph prayers" use a few, simple words to tell our urgent need or joy. I don't think the Lord expects beautiful, poetic words when we're in a crisis. I remember standing outside of a hospital X-ray room saying just, "Save her. Save her, please, save her."

Sometimes the crisis is one of personal survival. God also hears self-centered prayer, when survival is all that matters. As we work our way out of depression, we move thankfully from focusing on our own coping to noticing once more the needs of others around us. I speak from personal experience. What a blessed moment when we are able to reach out once more, stretch forth our hand in the pattern we learn from the Lord, to name the names of many others as we pray, seeking to bless their lives. One day recently I numbered the times I said, "Please bless *me*." It was appalling. I don't recommend that exercise. But if survival requires all our focus for a time, we can rejoice in the hope of a moment when we will lose our ego-centered view and see again the whole wide world and those who need our ministrations. We can then fill our prayers with the names of others.

Pray from the heart, a broken heart, a contrite spirit. It's our hearts that need to change and will change.

8. It was a splendid, starry night in the Caribbean, my first and last time on a small yacht. The next day we would fly home after one of the most spiritual weeks of my life, during which we had attended the dedication of the Washington Temple. I remember it now with just as much joy as I felt then. I think of it often when I need to remember; when I need to feel the Holy Ghost telling me again that it was a high point in my life. We were with beloved friends who had also attended the dedication, and the relaxed atmosphere and perfect weather were a great catalyst for long gospel conversations—a continuation of the Spirit we had felt at the temple.

One of those inspiring exchanges was in progress when I decided to go up on deck, just one more time, to see the stars. I climbed into a hammock and found myself totally alone under a magnificent canopy of stars. As I lay there in utter contentment, I

was gradually flooded with gratitude. I began to name the individual reasons for my joy, counting stars as I did. The stars seemed endless, and so did my thanks. As I catalogued each one, beginning
with Truman, I would add a sentence explaining one or more reasons for my joy. "Oh, Heavenly Father, I thank thee for Truman, for
his integrity, for his patience with me, for his fidelity to me in a
world where those words are almost unknown."

I warmed to the task, speaking aloud and at length about the
temple, my family, my friends, each one on the boat and all over the
world, my experiences one by one, and on and on, counting stars
and equating them with my gratitude. What had begun as a list of
blessings was continuing as a prayer. I soon realized this was the
longest prayer I had ever offered, and I felt no need to stop. When I
ran out of people, I counted sea and breezes and birds and flowers—
I described them, and I would have included those beautiful blue
flowers in England if I had known of them then. I even listed some
qualities in myself, talents with which I had been blessed. Somehow
it was easier to see them in this context. You can see how gratitude
can be contagious.

Then I began to realize how I prized my knowledge of the
Restoration and Joseph Smith. I had a lot to say about Joseph
Smith. It was only natural to chronicle my joy in the Savior and his
atoning for me. By then I was filled to the brim, and I didn't want
to stop. I understood how Enos and others could have prayed all
night. And with Enos I cried out in joy, "'Oh Lord, how is it
done?' How do you give me these feelings? How do I know the
feeling of the Holy Ghost?" I wanted this feeling of love and joy
never to end. But it did.

When we flew into Salt Lake the next evening, I was still trail-
ing the clouds of gratitude I had felt. Our bishop was waiting for us
in the rain. He had come to tell us that our Lamanite son had been

sent home from his mission and put on Church probation. I think that after expressing gratitude for Truman, my prayer the night before had moved to this son, "Thank you that after eleven years, Larry is serving in the mission field."

I learned then that counting blessings with all energy of heart can be a glorious, communing experience and that it will fill you with love. I also learned that the love fortifies us for the pain and disappointment that are a part of this earth life. To paraphrase, after great blessings, cometh the tribulation.

On the boat, praying felt easy and natural, but I have also learned to pray when I don't feel like it. Sometimes we feel unworthy to pray; we avoid the process because we feel unclean, out of sorts, angry, hostile, or just plain tired. How Satan must laugh as we *abandon praying* instead of hurrying to our knees to be cleansed and nurtured.

"Prayer changes things" reads a little sign sitting in the bookcase of my childhood home. I learned there that prayer is our pathway to mighty changes. When you don't feel like praying, read the words of the Lord. Read Jesus' tender invitation, "Come unto me, all ye that labour and are heavy laden, and I will give you rest" (Matthew 11:28.) Come, he says over and over. Through Alma he implores us, "Come and fear not, and lay aside every sin, which easily doth beset you, . . . and show unto your God that ye are *willing* to repent of your sins and enter into a covenant with him." (Alma 7:15; emphasis added.) The desire to pray will grow in you as you read the scriptures, and you will be able to close the book with renewed desire to speak with the author.

9. To say "Thy will be done" in matters of life and death, and mean it, requires tremendous faith and courage. Several years ago our youngest daughter was literally bleeding to death just after her last child was delivered. Truman rushed to the hospital to help administer to her. I was left alone in her home with two sleeping

grandchildren. Her newborn son slept in the hospital nursery. All three were oblivious to the fact that their mother was seriously at risk. But I wasn't. I paced and prayed and cried and gazed out into the black night.

"Thy will, *not mine,* be done." We mouth the words easily until someone we love deeply is at risk. I found it impossible even to mouth the words then, just in case it was *not* his will for her to live. At such moments we plead, "claiming" our imagined merit or theirs; we bargain with the Lord, not unlike Abraham as he bargained for a handful of the righteous in ancient, wicked cities. Sometimes, after the flailing around is finished, we sink again to our knees and whisper as quietly as we can, "Not my will but thine be done," barely able to muster the faith to say it.

I had not yet reached this point of submission. Instead, I paced and prayed, looked in on the children, and imagined various possible scenarios. Who could possibly love and support Grant as Mindy could? Who could rear those three little ones with the same dedication, inspiration, and flair? My agitation fed on itself, and I could see all would be better served if I focused my faith on the miracle needed. "Please stop the bleeding," I pleaded over and over, weeping as I spoke.

Then I learned what the Lord meant when he said, "Did I not speak peace to your mind concerning the matter? What greater witness can you have than from God?" (D&C 6:23.) In the midst of my churning emotions, an unmistakable calm came over me. "Everything is going to be all right." It was a clear message, but I quickly inserted into my running prayer, "But will she live?" because I knew everything could be all right but she could die. No answer. That's significant. No answer, but again, and with a serenity I have memorized, "Be at peace. Everything is going to be all right." And it was. She was anemic and weak for months but today is healthy and strong.

That same coin has another side, however. Not long ago our family combined our faith to pray for the healing of a beloved friend with cancer. We asked for a miracle. We pleaded for a miracle. But he died. During the long year of his illness, we exercised faith for his recovery, and at moments it seemed to be happening. But finally this strong man gave himself over to the will of the Lord. There was a purity and grace about him during his final days. I learned from him the meaning of sanctification. We prayed often together. He no longer asked for his life to be prolonged—he was forty-three years old with a wife and three young children—but he quietly assured the Lord that he wanted nothing more than to see the Lord's will done. He didn't pray for himself. He prayed for us and others whom he loved. I watched his own will being swallowed up in the will of our Heavenly Father. So I began to exercise the faith that I hoped would prolong his life to aid him in this sacred process.

It has been a while since he died. I watched and learned, but I still struggle to understand God's purposes, to align my will with his. The process continues in me. I do not doubt God's wisdom, but I struggle to understand, to make that wisdom my own. I know that bringing that struggle to the Lord in prayer is my avenue to peace.

Life-and-death experiences continue to tutor me. I learned in those crisis times to "pray with all energy of heart." What other way was there? I learned to focus in ways I had never dreamed possible. That kind of prayer takes an amazing amount of energy and endurance and patience. I don't always manage it. We "underpray" far more often than we "overpray," skimming the surface, seldom dipping heart-deep. But I know now how it feels. How we can learn to look up! Reach up! Pray through tears. Pray steadfastly, patiently, but look up! (See Russell M. Nelson, "Thou Shalt Have No Other Gods," *Ensign,* May 1996, 14–16.)

The words of the prophet Micah come to me readily when I find myself looking down. "Therefore I will look unto the Lord; I will wait for the God of my salvation: my God will hear me. Rejoice not against me, O mine enemy: when I fall, I shall arise; when I sit in darkness, the Lord shall be a light unto me." (Micah 7:7–8.) Don't rejoice, Mr. Devil. I may be down, but I'm not out! We can only be defeated if we refuse to get up, to look up, to reach up!

Isaiah teaches us that the Lord constantly reaches to us as he repeats over and over again, "His hand is stretched out still"—not just "out" but "stretched out." (See, for example, Isaiah 5:25; 9:12, 17, 21; 10:4.) How often the Lord asks throughout the book of Isaiah, "Is my arm too short to save you?" and the rhetorical question is answered with a resounding, "No!" We are his work and his glory. We are his first concern. We are, after all, his children. If we stretch to him, we will reach him. I picture the hands on the ceiling of the Sistine Chapel, all but touching. He longs to touch, grasp, and lift us to him.

These are the ideas about prayer that I hoped would be most helpful to you. I could go on and tell you how my mother taught me to love the words of St. Francis: "Lord, make me an instrument of thy peace."[1] She taught me that *all* people can know how to pray and approach God, not just Latter-day Saints.

Or, I'd tell you of sublime answers when I have prayed to be an instrument in the Lord's hands. Or I would tell you about my ongoing prayers to perfect my relationship with my cherished husband so that the promises given to us would launch us from our fifty-three

1. Saint Francis of Assisi, "Make Me an Instrument of Thy Peace." See, for example, *Love Never Faileth: The Inspiration of Saint Francis, Saint Augustine, Saint Paul, and Mother Teresa,* by Eknath Easwaran (Petaluma, Calif.: Nilgiri Press, 1984), 18.

years so far into forever. Or I would tell you about the gentle guidance that came to me in answer to my prayers about this chapter.

Mormon spoke the words which are my theme. Quoted by his son, Moroni, Mormon's words are the climax of a great sermon on charity, the pure love of Christ. "Pray unto the Father with all the energy of heart, that ye may be filled with this love, which he hath bestowed upon all who are true followers of his Son, Jesus Christ; that ye may become the sons [and daughters] of God; that when he shall appear we shall be like him, for we shall see him as he is; that we may have this hope; that we may be purified even as he is pure." (Moroni 7:48.) I know that we receive the Spirit through prayer and are thus given access to Christlike love. Our lives—mind, body, and spirit—are renewed in this process of sacred communion, and we become like him and like our Father in Heaven who loves and reaches out to each of us.

> *Lord, make me an instrument of thy peace.*
> *Where there is hatred, let me sow love;*
> *Where there is injury, pardon;*
> *Where there is doubt, faith;*
> *Where there is despair, hope;*
> *Where there is darkness, light;*
> *Where there is sadness, joy.*
> *O divine Master, grant that I may not so much seek*
> *To be consoled as to console,*
> *To be understood as to understand,*
> *To be loved as to love:*
> *For it is in giving that we receive,*
> *It is in pardoning that we are pardoned,*
> *It is in dying to self that we are born to eternal life.*

Family

Prayer

PRESIDENT SPENCER W. KIMBALL

A PROMINENT WRITER and marriage counselor has written: "Strong family life is indispensable, not merely to the culture but actually the survival of any people. In the history of mankind one nation after another has followed this pattern [of degrading family life and substituting other patterns for it] and they [have] disappeared. . . . For the well being of the community; for the very existence of the nation, one of the first questions asked about any proposed change in the culture should be, 'Will it strengthen the family?'" (Paul Popenoe, *Family Life,* September 1972.)

The Lord organized the whole program in the beginning, with a father who procreates, provides, and loves and directs, and a mother who conceives and bears and nurtures and feeds and trains. The Lord could have organized it otherwise, but he chose to have a unit with responsibility and purposeful associations where children train and discipline each other and come to love, honor, and appreciate each other. The family is the great plan of life as conceived and organized by our Father in heaven.

To any thoughtful person it must be obvious that intimate association without marriage is sin; that children without parenthood and family life is tragedy; that society without basic family life is without foundation and will disintegrate into nothingness and oblivion.

The Father knew all this when he gave this command to his children in November 1831. He was not arguing that there should be families. He seemed to take that for granted, and commanded: "Inasmuch as parents have children in Zion, . . . they shall also teach their children to pray, and to walk uprightly before the Lord." (D&C 68:25, 28.)

Once when I talked to leaders in a foreign country where different ideologies touch their children, I asked how the parents were able to hold their children and keep them from evil. Their reply was so natural and so proper:

"We train our children in our homes so completely in the way of right and truth that the destructive, godless philosophies and heresies of their other teachers run off without penetrating, like water on a duck's back, and our children remain true to the faith."

Ah, that is the answer. Family life, home life, home evenings, dedicated, selfless parents. That is the way the Lord ordained our lives to be.

More than a decade ago a major in the U.S. Air Force told of his test flights. He was born of goodly parents who taught him righteousness. He had flown twenty-five different types of military aircraft in four thousand hours in the air. He had flown 142 combat missions and had received many distinguished medals. He told us that "before takeoff every pilot takes a few moments to make a last-minute check of his engine, flight controls, hydraulic and pneumatic systems and other essential subsystems of his aircraft to be sure the flight can at least begin safely. . . . His reactions to emergency conditions must be as instinctive and as infallible as human thought and reflexes permit.

" . . . Yet, there is something missing on the printed checklist which to me has become as necessary to a successful flight as lowering the wheels for a smooth landing. It is a prayer to ask my Father in heaven to bless me that my best judgment and skill will guide my actions, especially in periods of stress. There have been several instances . . . in which I know the answer to this prayer has been received with dramatic suddenness."

Being born of goodly parents in a goodly home with goodly training in his infancy, childhood, and youth, he seemed to feel secure in his hazardous work. He was unafraid, for he was prepared. He knew the power of the Lord's statement: "If ye are prepared ye shall not fear." (D&C 38:30.)

That preparation comes from infancy and childhood training, when faith is born and character established. If children are tuned in on the right wavelength, if they are taught early the responsibilities of time and eternities, they will usually react properly when engulfed in emergencies. If they have consciously and faithfully done all that is expected of them, nothing can be too far wrong. The Nephite prophet insisted: "Ye must pour out your souls in your closets, and your secret places; and in your wilderness." (Alma 34:26.)

And what a great legacy to our children Isaiah promised: "And all thy children shall be taught of the Lord; and great shall be the peace of thy children." (Isaiah 54:13.)

Surely every good parent would like this peace for his offspring. It comes from the simple life of the true Latter-day Saint as he makes his home and family supreme.

"Pray in your families unto the Father, always in my name, that your wives and your children may be blessed." (3 Nephi 18:21.)

Is that too much to ask?

I was once in Idaho Falls, Idaho, as a guest in the home of a typical Latter-day Saint family. There was a dedicated set of parents and many children. The oldest was in military service in the South Pacific, and the hearts of the family followed him from place to place. They handed me his latest letter from the war zone. This is what I read:

"There have been times when we were so scared, we would tremble, but the fear was out of our minds with prayer and the knowledge that we were being guided by the Lord. Dad, I love my religion and I am proud that I had someone like you and Mother to teach me to pray. Then I also know that you are praying for me each morning and night."

Spirituality is born in the home and is nurtured in home evenings, in twice-a-day and oftener daily prayers, in weekly meetings when the family goes to church together. That spirituality as the foundation of one's life comes to his rescue when emergency strikes.

Security is not born of inexhaustible wealth, but of unquenchable faith. And generally that kind of faith is born and nurtured in the home and in childhood.

From World War II comes a story of a young Utah boy who was called to serve his country in the faraway places across several time zones. On his wrist he wore the conventional wristband watch to tell him the time in the area in which he was living. But strangely enough he carried a larger, heavier, old-time watch in his pocket, which gave another time of day. His buddies noted that frequently he would look at his wristwatch, then turn to the old-fashioned one in his pocket, and this led them, in their curiosity, to ask him why the additional watch. Unembarrassed, he promptly said:

"The wristwatch tells me the time here where we are, but the big watch which Pa gave me tells me what time it is in Utah. You see," he continued, "mine is a large family—a very close family. When the big watch says 5 A.M. I know Dad is rolling out to milk the cows. And any night when it says 7:30, I know the whole family is around a well-spread table on their knees thanking the Lord for what's on the table and asking Him to watch over me and keep me clean and honorable. It's those things that make me want to fight when the goin' gets tough. . . . I can find out what time it is here easy enough. What I want to know is what time it is in *Utah.*" (Adapted from Vaughn R. Kimball, "The Right Time at Home," *Reader's Digest,* May 1944, 43.)

I knew this family well. I knew this sailor slightly. I knew this father. His cows had to feed a large family, but his greater interest was the growing children who needed more than milk and bread. I have knelt in mighty prayer with this wonderful family. The home training has carried through to the eternal blessing of this large family.

O my beloved brothers and sisters, what a world it would be if the members of every family in this church were to be on their knees like this every night and morning! And what a world it would be if hundreds of millions of families in this great land and other lands were praying for their sons and daughters twice daily. And what a world this would be if a billion families throughout the world were in home evenings and church activity and were on their physical knees pouring out their souls for their children, their families, their leaders, their governments!

This kind of family could bring us back toward the translation experience of righteous Enoch. The millennium would be ushered in. Enoch was asked questions about himself. He answered, among other things, "My father taught me in all the ways of God." (Moses 6:41.) And Enoch walked with God and he was *not,* for God took him.

Enoch and his people dwelt in righteousness in the city of Holiness, even Zion. And Zion was taken up into heaven.

Yes, here is the answer: righteous, teaching parents; obedient, loving children; faithfulness to family duties. These qualities in a home make for security and character in the lives of children.

Teaching Our Children to Pray

Elder Vaughn J. Featherstone

THE FAMILY UNIT IS truly the most important organization in time or eternity. President David O. McKay said, "No other success can compensate for failure in the home." (Conference Report, Apr. 1964, 5.) President Harold B. Lee declared, "The greatest work you will do will be within the walls of your own home." (*Ensign,* July 1973, 98.)

I believe that every young person has a basic belief in prayer. As parents we, by our example, need to teach our children how to pray, to provide lifelong stability and security for them. Children who see other members of the family go to the Lord in prayer learn to rely on communion with Heavenly Father when they themselves are in need.

I did not grow up in a home where we were taught to pray nor where we had family prayer. My father, though he was a member of the Church, was inactive, and my mother joined the Church when we children were older. As a young boy of eight or nine I recall being invited to attend Primary. I well remember the lessons on prayer. I did not know how to pray, so I memorized the Lord's Prayer. Sometimes I felt as if I needed to say it several times before I got through to Heavenly Father. What a blessing it would have been if I had been taught how to pray properly! How I wish I had been taught the four simple parts to prayer, which our Primary teachers today teach:

1. We address our Father in heaven.
2. We express our gratitude and love for him.
3. We ask for special blessings.
4. We close our prayers in the name of Jesus Christ.

Such prayers, simple and sweet, are heard. As we grow older, we never come to the end of growth in our ability to pray. Changing conditions in our health, work, personal welfare, perplexities, frustrations, discouragements, and needs increase the intensity of our prayers. What a sweet experience for young children or teenagers to join with us in our family prayers! What a blessing it is for them to know that their private, individual prayers are heard and answered by a kind, wise, loving Heavenly Father, and that they can take their problems—no matter how simplistic they may be—to him in prayer!

My wife and I have seven children, six sons and a daughter. Each one of our children has been taught to pray as soon as he or she was old enough to kneel. Some of the sweetest prayers ever offered in our home have been those of our children. Many times we as adults forget how teachable children are, and how much they can learn if we give them guidance and encouragement. Sometimes parents are overly permissive or too lax in their teaching, thinking their children do not comprehend. They comprehend more than we would suppose. They can be taught to pray at a very early age.

My wife, Merlene, has knelt with our little ones in prayer and has taught them specific things to say, concepts that will be a strength to them all their lives. For example, our son, Paul, who is just two and a half, has been saying little prayers for nearly a year now. He has been kneeling since he was about nine or ten months old. (Of course someone had to hold him.)

We always pray for other members of the family. Each prayer also includes these words: "Heavenly Father, help us to be prepared and worthy to go on missions. Help us to be pure and worthy to be married in the temple." Merlene is teaching Paul to always include the words, "Heavenly Father, I love thee and I know that thou dost love me." What a marvelous strength those words will be in times of testing or trial!

Heavenly Father is accessible to us all, both young and old. In my own life there have been moments when I have felt an overwhelming, absolute need for intervention by a kind Father in heaven. Our children learn great trust in prayer as we share with them these personal experiences.

When our fifth son, Lawrence, was born, my wife had complications in labor, and the doctor stayed by her side all day. She also had had a dream that frightened her. She dreamed that two men in black clothes had come to get her, and she feared this may have been a warning she might not make it through the delivery. Late that night the doctor asked me to leave the room so he could examine her again. Greatly concerned about her, I went out into the hall, stood by a window looking over the twinkling lights of the Salt Lake Valley, and, with tears in my eyes, pleaded with the Lord to spare her life.

While I was praying, someone came rushing down the hallway. I saw a nurse run into my wife's room, then come out, get a cart with a tank of oxygen, and wheel the cart into the room. Now I knew my wife was in great danger. Although I thought I had been praying with all my heart, I suddenly found I could pray with even greater humility and pleading. I promised the Lord I would do anything I was ever asked to do in the Church if he would spare Merlene's life. The prayer was offered with every particle of my being.

In a few moments the door opened, and they were wheeling her to the delivery room. Lawrence, weighing ten pounds and twelve ounces, was born shortly after, and his mother soon recovered her health. Our prayers had been answered.

When Lawrence was thirteen we were expecting our seventh child, and again I was concerned for my wife's well-being. I tried not to alarm my family. However, I had told Lawrence about some of the difficulties connected with his birth, and this affected him greatly.

When I took Merlene to the hospital I told the family I would call them and let them know how their mother was and whether they had a little brother or sister. After Paul was born, I called home and Lawrence answered. I told him the good news and said I would be home in a little while. When I went home I told them all about their new baby brother and that their mother was doing well. That evening as I left the house to go to the hospital, Lawrence handed me a letter to give to his mother. When I arrived, I gave her a kiss, then handed her the letter. Her eyes moistened as she read it; then she handed it to me. It said:

"To my favorite and most loved Mother. Congratulations. When Dad phoned us and told us we had a little brother I just about freaked. After you left to go to the hospital I went in Dad's den and knelt down to have prayer to ask Heavenly Father to bless you that you would be all right. Well my prayer was answered. After Dad came home he told how just before the baby was born you gritted your teeth and tears flowed down your cheeks but you wouldn't cry out. I kind of got this unstuckable lump in my throat.

"I'm working on my hiking merit badge.

"Love, Lawrence"

Faith is often more pure in our children than it is in us. As adults, we tend to justify our lack of faith with our sense of practicality. Oftentimes we unthinkingly raise questions and doubts that lead them to modify their faith to our level of lesser faith. But children have a sweet, unquestioning trust in Heavenly Father, and we need to help them nurture this simple faith.

When our second son, Dave, was twelve years old, he was home alone one afternoon when the telephone rang. It was one of the Laurels in our ward who was calling. Her car had a flat tire and she had been unable to find anyone to help her fix it, so she called to see if my wife, who was president of the Young Women of the ward, could help her. Dave said, "I'm home alone, but I can ride my bike and help you change the tire." When he hung up the phone, he remembered he hadn't asked her where she was. He went into his bedroom, knelt down, and asked the Lord to take him to this girl. Then he went out, climbed on his bicycle, and rode directly to where she was.

In my own life I recall an experience in my boyhood that made a lasting impression on me. May I share it with you.

When I was a deacon in the Aaronic Priesthood, the member of the bishopric who advised the deacons quorum came into our quorum meeting the Sunday before Thanksgiving and said, "I hope we won't have one member of this quorum who won't kneel down in family prayer and have a blessing on the food this Thanksgiving." It was 1943, and our country was engaged in World War II. We discussed our need for a divine blessing for those who were in military service and for all the other difficulties we as a nation were facing. We also talked about the blessings we each enjoyed. Then we were again encouraged to have family prayer.

A heavy cloud settled on my heart. I didn't know how our family could have family prayer. My father had a drinking problem, and my mother was not a member of the Church at that time. We had never had a prayer in our home, not even a blessing on the food. After quorum meeting I continued to consider the challenge, and finally concluded we would not be able to have prayer.

That evening at sacrament meeting the bishop stood up at the close of the meeting and said, "Brothers and sisters, Thursday is Thanksgiving. I hope we will not have one family in the ward that will not kneel in family prayer. We ought to express our gratitude for the great goodness of our Heavenly Father to us." And then he enumerated some of our many blessings.

Again it seemed as if my soul was filled with an ominous gloom. I tried to figure out a way our family could have prayer. I thought about it Monday, and again on Tuesday, and on Wednesday. On Wednesday evening my father did not return home from work at the normal hour, and I knew from experience that, because it was payday, he was satisfying his thirst for alcohol. When he finally came at two in the morning quite an argument ensued. I lay in bed wondering how we could ever have prayer with that kind of contention in our home.

On Thanksgiving morning, we did not eat breakfast so we could eat more dinner. My four brothers and I went out to play with some neighbor boys. We decided to dig a hole and make a trench to it and cover it over as a clubhouse. We dug a deep hole, and with every shovelful of dirt I threw out of the hole I thought about family prayer for Thanksgiving. I wondered if I would have enough courage to suggest to my parents that we have a prayer, but I was afraid I would not. I wondered if my older brother, who has always been an ideal in my life, would suggest it, since he had been in the same sacrament meeting and had heard the bishop's suggestion.

Finally, at about 2:30 in the afternoon, Mother told us to come get cleaned up for dinner. Then we sat down at the big round oak table. Dad sat down with us silently—he and Mother were not speaking to each other. As she brought in the platter with the beautiful golden brown turkey, my young heart was about to burst. I thought, *Now please, won't someone suggest we have a family prayer?* I thought the words over and over, but they wouldn't come out. I turned and looked at my older brother, praying desperately that he would suggest prayer. The bowls of delicious food were being passed around the table; plates were being filled; and time and opportunity were passing. I knew that if someone did not act immediately, it would be too late. Then suddenly, as always, everyone just started eating.

My heart sank, and despair filled my soul. Although I had worked up a great appetite, and Mother was a marvelous cook, I wasn't hungry. I just wanted to pray.

I resolved that day that no son or daughter of mine would ever want to pray and not be able to do it because of shyness or lack of courage. In our family we have family prayers, personal prayers, and blessings on every meal. As one who has known the contrast between families that do not pray and those that do, I know the value of prayer in the home and in the life of every child and youth in the Church.

It is good to share with our children faith-promoting stories that teach them how to respond to answers to prayer and listen to the promptings of the Spirit. One such story is the one President Harold B. Lee told, of how as a young boy he decided he would go to a neighbor's property to explore an old building. As he climbed through the fence he heard a voice telling him not to go over there. He obediently responded and did not continue on. Because of his obedience he may never know what the price of disobedience would have been. We need to teach our children that it is better not to find out than to experience the consequences of disobedience. Satan uses curiosity in us all to tempt us and lead us in his directions. There are some things we don't need to know. President Lee did not need to know why he should stay away from the old building.

Some time ago a couple came to my office with very heavy hearts. They had a son who was of priest age, an Eagle Scout, a Duty to God Award winner, a good student who had been conscientious in school and on his part-time job. Then one night he just walked away from home and didn't return. He had been gone for several weeks, and they were heartsick.

I asked them if they had pleaded with the Lord to know where their son was. They assured me they had. "Have you pleaded with all your strength?"

"Yes, we have."

"Have you pleaded with every particle of your being?"

"Well," they said, "maybe not every particle."

I said, "You go home and pray again—this time with every particle of energy and strength of your being." They said they would.

That afternoon the couple knelt down at about three o'clock, and they spent one hour on their knees, pleading with the Lord. At six o'clock the phone rang. It was their son, calling from Banff, Alberta, Canada. After talking to him for a few minutes and finding that he was safe and in no danger, they asked why he had called at that particular time. He replied, "The bishop this evening had the strongest impression to have me call home. He came over to my apartment and said he would not leave until I called home."

We need to teach our children that some things demand pleading with the Lord. When we come to know that without his help we cannot possibly accomplish our desires, then we must learn to plead to whatever extent necessary.

As parents, we teach our children "to walk in the light" when we teach them to pray. Great blessings are wrought through prayer. The God of heaven would not expect us to pray to him if he had no intention of answering our prayers.

One of the choicest experiences of my life was to kneel in prayer with a mature couple in the office of President Spencer W. Kimball. I felt President Kimball's overpowering love for our Father in heaven as we knelt together. He taught us much about prayer through his example. We as parents ever and always will teach more by our example than by precept.

In summary, then, let me suggest that we need to teach our children to pray at the earliest possible age. They need to be taught to believe that answers to prayers truly are forthcoming. They need to see a lifelong example of parents who know how to pray. They need to understand that sometimes it takes pleading with the Lord to humble us to the dust of the earth before answers come. They need to learn that we should pray as though everything depended upon God, and then work as though everything depended upon us. When we follow through on our part of the agreement with our Heavenly Father, answers always come. And as parents, we can learn from our children the power that is found in simple, pure, unquestioning faith. May the Lord bless us as parents in fulfilling these sacred responsibilities.

Adversity
and Prayer

BISHOP H. BURKE PETERSON

A YOUNG MOTHER once said to me, "It seems in our home we go from one crisis to another. We never seem to be in calm waters. Either it's sick children, a Primary lesson to prepare, a car that breaks down before meetings, a flooded bathroom—you name it, we've had it." I suppose there are many whose life pattern would echo that refrain, even though the experiences will vary with each of us.

Because of the countless problems surrounding us and because of the trials and tribulations we are all confronted with, I've felt a need to be built up again in our understanding of why we have adversity and what we can do to weather its storm. It seems that life is filled with a variety of difficult experiences that test us and try us.

We should understand that a life filled with problems is no respecter of age or station in life. A life filled with trials is no respecter of position in the Church or social standing in the community. Challenges come to the young and to the aged, to the rich and to the poor, to the struggling student or the genius scientist, to the farmer, carpenter, lawyer, or doctor. Trials come to the strong and to the weak, to the sick and to the healthy. Yes, trials come even to the simplest child as well as to a prophet of God. At times they seem to be more than we can bear.

Now, some will say, "Why would a Father in heaven who calls us his children, who says he loves us above all of his creations, who says he wants only the best for us, who wants us to be happy and enjoy life to the fullest—why does he let these things happen to us, if we are really that dear to him?" The scriptures and the prophets have some needed answers for us.

We read in Helaman: "And thus we see that except the Lord doth chasten his people with many afflictions, yea, except he doth visit them with death and with terror, and with famine and with all manner of pestilence, they will not remember him." (Helaman 12:3.)

At a recent stake conference the stake president called a young father, who had just been ordained an elder, from the audience to bear his testimony. The father had been active in the Church as a boy, but during his teenage years he had veered somewhat from his childhood pattern. After returning from military service he married a lovely girl, and presently children blessed their home. Without warning an undisclosed illness overcame their little four-year-old daughter. Within a very short time she was on the critical list in the hospital. In desperation and for the first time in many years the father went to his knees in prayer, asking that her life be spared. As her condition worsened and he sensed that she would not live, the tone of the father's prayers changed; he no longer asked that her life be spared, but rather for a blessing of understanding: "Let thy will be done," he said. Soon the child was in a coma, indicating her hours on earth were few. Now, fortified with understanding and trust, the young parents asked for one more favor of the Lord. Would he allow her to awaken once more that they might hold her closely? The little one's eyes opened, her frail arms stretched out to her mother and then to her daddy for a final embrace. When the father laid her on the pillow to sleep till another morning, he knew their prayers had been answered—a kind, understanding Father in heaven had filled their needs as he knew them to be. His will had been done—they were determined now to live so that they might live again with her.

Do you remember the words of the Lord to the Prophet Joseph Smith when he was having that great test of his faith in the Liberty Jail? The Lord said, "If thou art called to pass through tribulation . . ." and he enumerated a series of possibilities that would test any man to the utmost. He then concluded: "Know thou, my son, that all these things shall give thee experience, and shall be for thy good." (D&C 122:5, 7.)

It's interesting to note that from the depths of trial and despair have come some of the most beautiful and classic passages of modern-day scripture—not from the ease of a comfortable circumstance. Might this also be the case in our own lives! From trial comes refined beauty.

We could cite Beethoven or Abraham Lincoln or Demosthenes who won out in a most difficult struggle to become a magnificent orator—but closer to us we see the great beauty and wisdom in the speaking and teaching of President Spencer W. Kimball, and we see the price he's paid that our lives might be blessed.

In speaking of the Savior, the scriptures tell us: "Though he were a Son, yet learned he obedience by the things which he suffered." (Hebrews 5:8.)

From Hebrews we also read: "My son, despise not thou the

chastening of the Lord, nor faint when thou art rebuked of him: for whom the Lord loveth he chasteneth, and scourgeth every son whom he receiveth." (Hebrews 12:5–6.)

Let us remember—trials are an evidence of our Father's love. They are given as a blessing to his children. They are given as opportunities for growth.

Now, how do we approach them? How do we overcome them? How are we magnified by them? There seems to be a reason why we lose our composure in adversity—why we think we can no longer cope with what we're faced with here in this life. There is a reason why we give up, why we "fall apart at the seams," so to speak. The reason may be so simple that we lose sight of it.

Could it be because we begin to lose contact with our greatest source of strength—our Father in heaven? He is the key to our enjoying sweetness in adversity—in gaining strength from our trials—he and he alone.

As a reassurance to us, let us read from the New Testament: "There hath no temptation taken you but such as is common to man: but God is faithful, who will not suffer you to be tempted above that ye are able; but will with the temptation also make a way to escape, that ye may be able to bear it." (1 Corinthians 10:13.)

Did you get the significance of that scriptural promise? We will have no temptation or trial beyond our ability to overcome. He will provide a way for us to rise above whatever the trial may be.

May I suggest that the best way I know to keep close to the source of this great strength is through prayer. No man can stand alone in his struggle through life. Sometimes in discouragement our prayers, at best, become occasional or maybe not at all. Sometimes we forget or just don't care.

Some may think that because they have a Word of Wisdom

problem or because they have been dishonest or immoral, because they have not prayed for years, because of many reasons, they are now unworthy. "It's too late. I've made so many mistakes—so why even try?" To these we say, "For your own sake, give yourself another chance."

Sincere prayer is the heart of a happy and productive life. Prayer strengthens faith. Prayer is the preparation for miracles. Prayer opens the door to eternal happiness. The Father of us all is personal, ever waiting to hear from us, as any loving father would his children. To learn to communicate with him, to learn to pray effectively, requires diligence and dedication and desire on our part. I wonder sometimes if we are willing to pay the price for an answer from the Lord.

As we learn to develop this two-way communication, the standard of our life will improve. We will see things more clearly; we will try harder to do better; we will see the real joy that can come through trials and testing. Although problems will still be with us, peace, contentment, and true happiness will be ours in abundance.

As you feel the need to confide in the Lord or to improve the quality of your visits with him—to pray, if you please—may I suggest a process to follow: go where you can be alone, where you can think, where you can kneel, where you can speak out loud to him. The bedroom, the bathroom, or a closet will do. Now, picture him in your mind's eye. Think to whom you are speaking. Control your thoughts—don't let them wander. Address him as your Father and your friend. Now tell him things you really feel to tell him—not trite phrases that have little meaning, but have a sincere, heartfelt conversation with him. Confide in him. Ask him for forgiveness. Plead with him. Enjoy him. Thank him. Express your love to him. Then listen for his answers. Listening is an essential part of praying. Answers from the Lord come quietly, ever so quietly. In fact, few hear his answers audibly with their ears. We must be listening carefully or we will never recognize them. Most answers from the Lord are felt in our heart as a warm, comfortable expression, or they may come as thoughts to our mind. They come to those who are prepared and who are patient.

Yes, the trials will still be there; but with the companionship of the Spirit, our approach to trials will change frustrations and heartaches to blessings.

Just for a moment, think with me. Forget the trials you now have. Remember back to those trials you had last year, five years ago, ten years ago. What did you gain? What did you learn? Aren't you better prepared now because of them?

I testify the Lord is ready and waiting to help us. For our own good we must take the first step, and this step is prayer.

Pray Always
and Be Believing

CAROLYN J. RASMUS

FROM THE TIME I was a young child I have believed in prayer. My parents taught me about it, I heard others pray, and it has always seemed like the right thing to do. I have heard many bear testimony that their prayers have been answered—that they have found their way when they have been lost, received guidance on an important decision, or found a way to relate to one of their children who seemed lost and alienated from the family. I also know people who feel frustrated and even guilty because they have prayed with all of their soul and yet have sensed no guidance on important matters. They begin to question their own faith, the "rightness" of their prayer, or even if God exists.

The scriptures are clear on our responsibilities concerning prayer. Repeatedly we are admonished to "pray always." (See 2 Nephi 32:9; Alma 13:28; 3 Nephi 18:18; D&C 10:5; D&C 88:126; Matthew 26:41; Mark 13:33; Luke 21:36.) The scriptures also contain numerous and repeated references to Christ, our Exemplar, praying to the Father. Likewise, the scriptures are filled with examples of others who prayed to God for a variety of reasons—to praise God, to express thanks, to seek for guidance, to be healed, to receive comfort, to resist temptation, to plead for forgiveness, to experience patience, to seek a blessing such as relief from drought, and so forth. Many people have written about prayer—how to pray, when to pray, the appropriate language of prayer, and how to prepare ourselves to pray.

For all I have come to know and experience about prayer, there have been times when I've still had many questions about this form of communication with our Father. Why is it that sometimes answers seem to come so clearly, almost before we've said the prayer, and yet at other times, after intensive and persistent pleadings with the Lord, we feel we are left on our own? Does receiving an answer one time and not another mean we pray with more faith sometimes? Does it mean that at times we are seeking the wrong, or an unrighteous, blessing?

Our Relationship to Heavenly Father

One day when earnestly seeking to better understand prayer and to make it more meaningful in my own life, I read the following statement in the Bible Dictionary: "As soon as we learn the true relationship in which we stand toward God (namely, God is our Father, and we are his children), then at once prayer becomes natural and instinctive on our part. Many of the so-called difficulties about prayer arise from forgetting this relationship." (LDS Edition of the King James Version, "Bible Dictionary," 752.)

Suddenly my mind was flooded with thoughts. Although we cannot remember the time prior to our earthly birth, we do know that we are the spirit children of Heavenly Parents. We lived with them, were taught by them, and had opportunities to commune with them. If we were to become perfect, it was necessary for us to leave our Heavenly Father and our premortal home, and come to earth. When we were born of mortal parents, a veil covered our spiritual eyes, and we could no longer remember our pre-earth experiences.

God endowed man with "agency." (Moses 7:32.) With this agency, man became free to choose "liberty and eternal life" or "captivity and death." (2 Nephi 2:27.) We are to be "tried in all things" (D&C 136:31) to "see if [we] will do all things whatsoever the Lord [our] God shall command [us]." (Abraham 3:25.)

The plan was not that we would be sent to earth and left on our own. The first instruction the Lord gave Adam and Eve after they were driven from the Garden of Eden was to pray. (See Moses 5:5.) In other words, through prayer man, though physically separated from God, could continue to commune with him.

The desire of our Heavenly Father is for us to ultimately return to him. Anticipating the fall of Adam and Eve, God provided a Redeemer to rescue us from the Fall and to show us a perfect example of how to live so that we might become more godly. As I thought about this great plan of salvation, several things became very clear to me: I am *literally* a spirit child of my heavenly parents; I lived with them, I knew them, and they knew me well; to grow in wisdom and knowledge and judgment, it was necessary for me to leave my Heavenly Parents and come to earth and receive an earthly body; I was given agency—I can make choices and will learn from them; the plan is for me to ultimately return to my Heavenly Father; this is made possible through the Atonement of Christ. Through his life I can learn how to live my life. I have not been left here on the earth alone with no knowledge of who I am or why I am here. The scriptures teach me about these things. They also teach me about God and what he is like and of his concern for me.

Communicating with Our Father

As these thoughts came to my mind I began to more clearly understand the purpose of prayer. It is the means by which I have continued opportunities to call upon and talk with my Heavenly Father, now that I am no longer in his presence. Because I believe that he is all-knowing and that he knows me better than I know myself—as earthly parents often know their children better than the children know themselves—I know that he will respond to me in ways that are best for me.

When we come to understand that prayer is our means of access to God our Father, we become increasingly more comfortable in calling upon him. When we know that our Father knows us and hears us and responds to us, we will be anxious to "commune" with him. (See Exodus 25:22.) It is then that we will put aside "vain repetitions" (3 Nephi 13:7) and pour out our whole souls to God. (Enos 1:9; Mosiah 24:12) Ultimately, we will be more anxious to listen than to rehearse our own litany of lists.

When we consider God as our loving Father, who desires to help and bless us, our desire to commune with him will increase. Christ said to his disciples: "Ask, and it shall be given you; seek, and ye shall find; knock, and it shall be opened unto you." (Luke 11:9.) That instruction seems clear enough, but what follows gives us great insight concerning our Father in Heaven: "If a son shall ask bread of any of you that is a father, will he give him a stone? or if he ask a fish, will he for a fish give him a serpent? Or if he shall ask an egg, will he offer him a scorpion? If ye then, being evil, know how to give good gifts unto your children: how much more shall your heavenly Father give the Holy Spirit to them that ask him?" (Luke 11:11–13.)

These scriptures relate a father responding to a son to our Heavenly Father responding to us. Often a child asks for something, but either because of experience or knowledge or understanding (of the child and/or the situation), the parent does not give the child what he asks for. This may occur because the request is not in the child's best interest, or because of the parent's love for the child. Sometimes in being given "bread" the child perceives he is really receiving "a stone."

I remember one occasion when I was babysitting my younger brother, who was about sixteen months old. He'd wandered out of my sight, and after several minutes of not hearing him I went to investigate. He had managed to climb up a chair and onto the cupboard. There he sat, as proud as he could be of his accomplishment, happily playing with a shiny and very sharp butcher knife. Even though I was only twelve years old, I knew enough to take the knife away from him before he hurt himself. He immediately began to cry. He had been attracted to the knife because it was bright and shiny; to him, it was a plaything. But no matter how hard he cried, I would not give it to him. Now, some forty years later, I would not take a knife away from my brother. His own experience and judgment have matured to the point that he can handle a butcher knife without inflicting harm to himself.

Even though there were times I "thought I would die" if my parents did not grant me what I thought I had to have, I'm grateful for their wisdom in denying my request. Likewise, I can now see that many of the things for which I prayed at an earlier age would have been to my detriment or deprived me of growth if they had been granted the way I wanted and expected.

All of our prayers *are* answered, though sometimes not in the way we anticipate (and in retrospect, how grateful we can be that they are not.)

Even the Savior's prayer in Gethsemane was answered in the negative. In addition to learning that prayers are not always answered as we wish them to be, we learn two other important lessons from the Savior's experience. First, following his prayer we are told that an angel appeared unto him, strengthening him. Sometimes when we wish for a certain situation to be resolved or made right or prevented from happening, it is in our own best interest to be blessed instead with peace or understanding or additional knowledge or comfort or courage or increased faith or strength to bear up. Our Heavenly Father, who is all-knowing, all-wise, and who loves us very much, will always answer our prayers!

Not My Will, but Thine

The second thing we learn from Christ's prayer in Gethsemane is that he prayed, "Nevertheless not my will, but thine, be done." (Luke 22:42.) What a lesson for those of us who desire to be Christlike. Christ desired to do the Father's will. Even in the premortal life we have record of Christ, the Beloved Son, saying, "Father, thy will be done, and the glory be thine forever." (Moses 4:2.)

On numerous occasions Christ told us, "I seek not mine own will, but the will of the Father which hath sent me." (John 5:30; see also 3 Nephi 27:13; D&C 19:24.) He who exemplified by his life his desire to do the Father's will taught us, "Not every one that saith unto me, Lord, Lord, shall enter into the kingdom of heaven; but he that doeth the will of my Father which is in heaven." (Matthew 7:21; see also 3 Nephi 14:21.) Like Christ, the prophets have prayed, "Thy will, O Lord, be done, and not mine." (Jacob 7:14; Alma 14:13.)

Often it is shortsightedness that causes us to question whether God hears our prayers, or to believe that our prayers are unanswered. We lack the perspective of our Heavenly Father. Knowing only our mortal existence, we often fail to see things in an eternal perspective.

Following his address at the Sermon on the Mount (and the similar discourse given to the Nephites), the Savior taught the disciples how to pray and concluded by giving them an example that has come to be known as the Lord's prayer. (See Matthew 6 and 3 Nephi 13.) In both instances, the disciples were instructed to pray to their Father "who art in heaven" and to pray that "thy will be done in earth, as it is in heaven." (Matthew 6:9–10; 3 Nephi 13:9–10.)

In Christ's instructions concerning how we are to pray, he indicates that our "Father knoweth what things [we] have need of, before [we] ask him." (Matthew 6:8; 3 Nephi 13:8.) Why then do we pray at all? I believe it is because as we go through the process of using words to express ideas, we are forced to clarify our thinking and, in most instances, come to a new and clearer understanding.

In the early stages of work to achieve my doctoral degree, I had what I thought was a brilliant idea for a dissertation and was anxious to talk it over with my advisor. I made an appointment, arrived at her office at the appointed hour, and told her my purpose in coming. She asked to see my written proposal and an outline of what research I wanted to do.

"I don't have anything in writing yet," I responded. She dismissed me from her office and told me she would be glad to talk with me when I had something in writing.

I perceived her actions to be inappropriate and cruel. Yet, in the days that followed I discovered, as I struggled to put my thoughts into words, that I had not carefully thought through what I wanted to do. In fact, as a result of this exercise, I determined on my own that my idea would not be appropriate for a dissertation.

Often it is as we commune with our Heavenly Father through prayer that things become clear in our own minds. As we commune with him and seek to have his will done in our lives, we take time to reflect on the counsel and instruction he has already given us through the scriptures. In fact, Christ tells us that when "my words abide in you, ye shall ask what ye will, and it shall be done unto you." (John 15:7.)

The Lord told Nephi, son of Helaman, that because "thou . . . hast not sought thine own life, but hast sought my will," whatever he asked would be done. Nephi knew the Lord's will and the Lord knew Nephi. He knew that Nephi would "not ask that which is contrary to my will." (Helaman 10:4–5.)

It is incumbent upon us to learn the will of the Father. Perhaps that is why Nephi told us to "feast upon the words of Christ; for behold, the words of Christ will tell you all things what ye should do." He also taught us that the Spirit can teach us to pray. (See 2 Nephi 32:3, 8.) This idea is reinforced in a revelation given through the Prophet Joseph Smith: "He that asketh in the Spirit asketh according to the will of God." (D&C 46:30.) Likewise, the Spirit helps us to pray. Paul taught, "We know not what we should pray for as we ought: but the Spirit itself maketh intercession for us with groanings which cannot be uttered." (Romans 8:26.)

Study It Out in Your Mind

In our desire to respond to the invitation to "ask," we need also to be mindful of the Lord's admonition to Oliver Cowdery. "You have not understood," the Lord said. "You have supposed that I would give it unto you, when you took no thought save it was to ask me." The Lord then explained that Oliver needed first to "study it out in [his] mind." (D&C 9:7–8.) In my own experience, whether in writing or preparing a talk or trying to solve a problem,

I have found President Spencer W. Kimball's statement to be true: "Perspiration must precede inspiration; there must be effort before there is excellence. We must do more than pray for . . . outcomes, though we must surely pray. We must take thought. We must make effort. We must be patient. We must be spiritual." (Spencer W. Kimball, *The Teachings of Spencer W. Kimball* [Salt Lake City: Bookcraft, 1982], 402.)

In many instances it is the *process* of searching and studying and struggling that becomes more beneficial than the answer itself. I had such an experience in responding as a member of the Young Women General Board to an assignment given by the Young Women General Presidency. Each board member was asked to give written expression to the Young Women logo. It was suggested that our thoughts be limited to one or two short paragraphs.

I was excited about the assignment and immediately thought of the torch representing the Light of Christ, of the need for young women to be "a light" in a dark world, and of the torch as a symbol for young women to become literal "standard bearers." I jotted down a list of ideas and words to serve as a springboard for my writing.

I awoke early the next Saturday morning, excited about putting my thoughts on paper. When I sat down to write, I felt impressed to go to the library. I looked up books under the words *torch* and *torch bearer* and was surprised by the variety of books related to these two words. I selected nearly thirty books from which I drew ideas and spent about four hours reading and making notes of phrases and words. Later, I reviewed scriptural references on light.

By early evening I finally felt prepared to write. I cleared everything off my desk and sat before a blank piece of paper. That's when the struggle began. Several hours later I had written only two paragraphs, which I didn't feel particularly good about. But the next morning when I awoke, many of the words I had written came to my mind in rhyme. Ultimately, the Lord used my preparation and work to fulfill a purpose I could not have foreseen. The words I wrote were later put to music and used to introduce the Young Women's logo in a satellite broadcast.

We must learn that the immediacy of an answer to our prayers, or the perceived "no answer," is always given in our best interests. A loving Heavenly Father responds to his children in ways that are best for them and for their growth. The scriptures tell us that he will give us that thing "which is right" and "that is expedient for [us]." (D&C 88:64.)

I have always been touched by the story of Amanda Smith. This incident took place following the massacre at Haun's Mill in October 1838. Many had been brutally killed, but Amanda survived and returned to the scene in search of her husband and three sons. From a distance she saw one of her older sons carrying a younger brother and she cried out, "Oh! My Alma is dead!" Her son replied, "No, mother, I think Alma is not dead. But father and brother Sardius are killed." Later Amanda was to record in her journal:

"What an answer was this to appal [sic] me! My husband and son murdered; another little son seemingly mortally wounded; and perhaps before the dreadful night should pass the murderers would return and complete their work!

"But I could not weep then. The fountain of tears was dry; the heart overburdened with its calamity, and all the mother's sense absorbed in its anxiety for the precious boy which God alone could save by his miraculous aid.

"The entire hip joint of my wounded boy had been shot away. Flesh, hip bone, joint and all had been ploughed out from the muzzle of the gun which the ruffian placed to the child's hip through the logs of the shop and deliberately fired.

"We laid little Alma on a bed in our tent and I examined the wound. It was a ghastly sight. I knew not what to do. It was night now. . . .

"The women were sobbing, in the greatest anguish of spirit; the children were crying loudly with fear and grief at the loss of fathers and brothers; the dogs howled over their dead masters and the cattle were terrified with the scent of the blood of the murdered.

"Yet was I there, all that long, dreadful night, with my dead and my wounded, and none but God as our physician and help." (Edward W. Tullidge, *The Women of Mormondom* [New York: Tullidge and Crandall, 1877], 122–28.)

Amanda, in her anguish, cried to her Heavenly Father as might a child in trouble cry to her earthly father. Her cry for help was simple, short, and to the point. From her faithful, believing heart she cried, "Oh my Heavenly Father, what shall I do? Thou seest my poor wounded boy and knowest my inexperience. Oh Heavenly Father, direct me what to do!" Immediately she received an answer and was directed as if by a voice.

"Nearby was a slippery-elm tree. From this I was told to make a slippery-elm poultice and fill the wound with it. . . . I removed the wounded boy to a house, some distance off the next day, and dressed his hip; the Lord directing me as before. I was reminded that in my husband's trunk there was a bottle of balsam. This I poured into the wound, greatly soothing Alma's pain. . . .

"So Alma laid on his face for five weeks, until he was entirely recovered—a flexible gristle having grown in place of the missing joint and socket, which remains to this day a marvel to physicians." (Tullidge, *The Women of Mormondom,* 122–28.)

There are many scriptures about prayer. All are instructive. They help us better understand prayer and how to pray and give us examples of those who prayed in a variety of situations and circumstances.

I sincerely believe that one of the "keys" to our prayers is to remember that we are praying to our Heavenly Father who loves us and wants the best for us. The more we become familiar with his power, his knowledge, and his ways, the more we will desire to seek to do his will.

Communion
with the Infinite

ROBERT L. MILLET

No PERSON ASCENDS the mountain of spirituality who does not lift his voice and his heart in prayer to the Almighty. We remember President David O. McKay's definition of spirituality: "Spirituality is the consciousness of victory over self, and of communion with the Infinite." (*True to the Faith* [Salt Lake City: Bookcraft, 1966], 244–45.)

Why do we pray? First, we believe our Heavenly Father is a Man of Holiness (Moses 6:57), a glorified and exalted Being to be sure, but a resurrected and redeemed Man who is literally the Father of our spirits. He knows us, one by one, and has infinite love and tender regard for each one of us. He has a physical body, parts, and passions. He feels. He yearns. He pains and sorrows for our struggles and our wanderings. He delights in our successes. He responds to petitions and pleadings. He is neither untouchable nor unapproachable. Thus our prayers allow us to express to God our needs, our challenges, our deepest feelings and desires, and to ask sincerely for his help. The more prayerful we become, the more dependent we are upon God, and thus the more trusting and reliant upon spiritual powers beyond our own. Prayer thus builds our spiritual strength by pointing us beyond our limited resources to him who has all power. In short, we pray to better understand who we are and who God is. We pray to better understand what we can do on our own and what we can do only with divine assistance.

Second, prayer allows us to communicate with Deity, to open ourselves to conversation with divinity. If indeed the quality of our lives is largely a product of the kinds of associations we enjoy, then we may rest assured that individuals who spend much time in prayer will in time blossom in personality, rise above pettiness, littleness of soul, and mortal jealousies and fears. We cannot have contact with influences that are degrading without being affected adversely, almost as though the degrading words and deeds become a part of us. On the other hand, if we regularly call upon God, pour out our soul in prayer, and yearn for genuine communion with Deity, we cannot help but be elevated and transformed by that association. The very powers of God, coming to us through his Holy Spirit, make us into men and women of purpose, of purity, and of power. In short, we pray in order to receive an infusion of power, to draw strength from an omnipotent Being.

> *Oh, may my soul commune with thee*
> *And find thy holy peace;*
> *From worldly care and pain of fear,*
> *Please bring me sweet release.*
>
> *Oh, bless me when I worship thee*
> *To keep my heart in tune,*

That I may hear thy still, small voice,
And, Lord, with thee commune.

Enfold me in thy quiet hour
And gently guide my mind
To seek thy will, to know thy ways,
And thy sweet Spirit find.

Lord, grant me thy abiding love
And make my turmoil cease.
Oh, may my soul commune with thee
And find thy holy peace.

> ("Oh, May My Soul Commune with Thee," *Hymns of The Church of Jesus Christ of Latter-day Saints* [Salt Lake City: The Church of Jesus Christ of Latter-day Saints, 1985], no. 123.)

There are certain barriers to communion with the Infinite, things that get in the way and prevent us from enjoying the kind of closeness with our Heavenly Father that we could have. Let me suggest but a few.

Surely no roadblock could be more prevalent than distraction and preoccupation. Sometimes we don't pray well because our minds and hearts are focused on other things. We are too prone to think of prayer as something within the spiritual realm and of religion as just another department of life. Communion with the Infinite requires discipline, and discipline requires making priorities. Obviously we need to chase wickedness out of our lives if we are to draw close to God in prayer. But, in addition, when it is time to pray, we must put aside the things of the world, even good things, in order to engage the greatest good. We do not rush into the divine presence, any more than we would rush into the office of the president of the Church or the president of the United

States. It is often helpful, before we begin to pray, to slow down, stop what we're doing, sit quietly, listen to inspiring music, read several verses of scripture, or ponder and reflect on things that matter most.

Another roadblock to an effective prayer life is duplicity, or trying to lead two lives. James explained that "a double minded man is unstable in all his ways." (James 1:8.) Thus we would suppose that a person who is worldly throughout the day would have great difficulty praying intently at night. Elder Howard W. Hunter observed: "Henry Ward Beecher once said: *'It is not well for a man to pray cream and live skim milk.'* . . . That was a century ago. There is now before us a danger that many may pray skim milk and live *that* not at all." (In Conference Report, October 1977, 79; italics in original.) Just as our lives are only as good as our prayers, so our prayers are only as good as our lives. That is, the more faithful we become in keeping the Lord's commandments and putting first things first in our lives, the more we open the doors of communication with the heavens and the more comfortable we feel with holy things and holy beings.

Perhaps one common shortcoming is to say our prayers regularly but to do so without much thought, reflection, or devotion, except when we suppose that we really need God's help. Yet we know that we need his help every moment of every day of our lives. As King Benjamin pointed out to his people, God "is preserving you from day to day, by lending you breath, that ye may live and move and do according to your own will, and even supporting you from one moment to another." (Mosiah 2:21.) Elder Hunter explained: "If prayer is only a spasmodic cry at the time of crisis, then it is utterly selfish, and we come to think of God as a repairman or a service agency to help us only in our emergencies. We should remember the Most High day and night—always—not only at times when all other assistance has failed and we desperately need help. If there is any element in human life on which we have a record of miraculous success and inestimable worth to the human soul, it is prayerful, reverential, devout communication with our Heavenly Father." (In Conference Report, October 1977, 79.) One practice that I have found particularly meaningful—especially when I find myself reciting words instead of communing with God—is to devote myself to a prayer in which I ask the Lord for absolutely nothing but instead express sincere gratitude for all my blessings. This kind of prayer pays remarkable dividends and settles the soul as few other things will.

Coach Vince Lombardi wisely remarked that fatigue makes cowards of us all. Fatigue also makes it extremely difficult to enjoy our prayers. Perhaps it is not always wise to make our prayers the last thing we do each day. It may be worthwhile occasionally to have prayer well before going to bed, while our mind and body are able to do more than utter a few well-worn and familiar phrases. There have been several times over the years when one of my children has talked me into watching a late movie with them, perhaps on a Friday night. Knowing that inevitably I would fall asleep, either on the floor or on the couch, more than once I have gone into my bedroom, closed the door, and had a meaningful prayer before going downstairs to watch the movie.

It is a marvelous thing—although perhaps we do not think about it very much—to be called upon to offer prayer in a public meeting. It is an honor to address the Almighty God, but it is a special honor to be asked to do so on behalf of a group of fellow believers. We damage ourselves spiritually and rob ourselves of a small but significant opportunity to grow when we decline such invitations to pray. Some refuse because they feel shy or afraid. They should take heart, for we are all in this together. No one of us has all of the answers, and no one of us has achieved such great spiritual heights that he or she is in a position to judge another's prayer, no matter how simple or halting it might be. Others may refuse to pray because they do not feel worthy to do so. With the exception of those who are under Church discipline and have thus been asked by priesthood leaders not to participate in public meetings, all are worthy to pray if called upon.

Nephi explained the source of an attitude that refuses to pray. "If ye would hearken unto the Spirit which teacheth a man to pray," he wrote, "ye would know that ye must pray; for the evil spirit teacheth not a man to pray, but teacheth him that he must not pray." (2 Nephi 32:8.) The officers of the Church are charged to "visit the house of each member, and exhort them to pray vocally and in secret and attend to all family duties." (D&C 20:47; see also v. 51.) Elsewhere the Savior instructs the Saints: "I command thee that thou shalt pray vocally as well as in thy heart; yea, before the world as well as in secret, in public as well as in private." (D&C 19:28; compare 23:6; 81:3.)

There are some things we ought to keep in mind when we pray vocally. My father was fond of saying that we should pray for the occasion, meaning that we ought to consider why we are gathered together, what is needed most, and how we might best express those needs to our Father in Heaven. For one thing, public prayers, with perhaps the exception of dedicatory prayers, are and should be relatively short.

There may be occasions when it is necessary to take more time in prayer than usual, but such is rarely the case in public meetings. Shauna and I still remember attending a missionary farewell more than twenty-five years ago for a couple who had been called to serve a full-time mission. A number of people were called upon to speak—those were the days when sacrament meetings were an hour and a half long—but Grandpa was not one of them. He was, however, asked to offer the opening prayer. I can still remember our two eldest children, who were just learning to bow their little heads and keep their eyes closed for more than a few seconds, glancing up with a puzzled look as the elderly gentleman spoke in great detail in his prayer of Christ, the different dimensions of the Atonement, and a variety of other doctrinal topics. The prayer, which lasted for seventeen minutes, seemed somewhat out of place. Our prayers are not sermons; they are not public discourses. They are addressed not to other Saints but to God. Elder Francis M. Lyman taught: "It is not necessary to offer very long and tedious prayers, either at opening or closing. It is not only not pleasing to the Lord for us to use excess of words, but also it is not pleasing to the Latter-day Saints. Two minutes will open any kind of meeting, and a half minute will close it." (Lyman, address delivered at MIA Conference, 5 June 1892; reprinted in *Improvement Era,* April 1947, 245.)

Two keys to meaningful prayer, including public prayer, are sincerity and simplicity. We have no one to impress, no one's judgment to fear. Our words are addressed to him who knows all things, including the desires of our hearts. (D&C 6:16.) It is thus wise to speak the words that we really feel. In Shakespeare's *Hamlet,* Claudius stopped praying because his heart was simply not in his prayers. He said, "My words fly up, my thoughts remain below; / Words without thoughts never to heaven go." (Act III, scene 3.) The Prophet Joseph Smith taught in regard to prayer, "Be plain and simple, and ask for what you want, just like you would go to a neighbor and say, 'I want to borrow your horse to go to the mill.'" (As cited in Helen Mae Andrus and Hyrum L. Andrus, *They Knew the Prophet* [Salt Lake City: Bookcraft, 1974], 100.) As a part of his own prayer to God, Zenos exclaimed, "Yea, thou art merciful unto thy children when they cry unto thee, to be heard of thee and not of men, and thou wilt hear them." (Alma 33:8.)

When we are called upon to pray, we should pray from our hearts with the dignity and respect due the God whom we are addressing. I am often pained as people hurry through a prayer as though it were a formality that needed to be dispensed with as quickly and painlessly as possible. That is particularly true for the end of the prayer. We should close our prayers with the dignity and transcendent respect that we ought to have for the name of him who bought us with his blood, the Savior of all mankind. Sometimes people are so eager to be finished with the prayer that they race through the name of Jesus Christ as though they were sprinting toward a finish line. That cannot be pleasing to his Father, who is also our Father. If we pray sincerely, from our hearts, speaking our words soberly and distinctly—especially the concluding words, "in the name of Jesus Christ"—we will begin to feel a power and a sacred influence in our lives that attests that the Lord hears us and is pleased with us.

One thing most needed in our prayer lives is consistency and regularity. Some people find it helpful to pray in the same place. One man I know set aside a special room in his home, a place which over the years came to be like his personal sacred grove. It seemed when he entered that room that he felt a hallowed presence. In fact, because some of the most profound insights and some of the sweetest feelings and impressions came to him in that room, it represented almost a holy of holies within his templed home.

Nearly forty years ago another man taught me something that changed my life. He said simply, "When you get out of bed in the morning, never let your feet touch the floor first. Always let your knees touch first." I recommend that bit of practical wisdom, especially if you find it difficult to have a regular, meaningful morning prayer. I have been surprised at how many people who would never consider going to bed without praying in the evening have not developed a consistent pattern of prayer in the mornings.

In practical terms, I have thought that there are very few harmful or hazardous things that could happen to me between the time I lay my head on the pillow at night and the time I get up, but there are many challenges and temptations and decisions I must face throughout the day, and I need all the help I can get. Evening prayers are extremely important, and morning prayers are vital.

Two of my colleagues at Brigham Young University, Brent Top and Bruce Chadwick, have told me that their studies of morality and faithfulness in Latter-day Saint youth throughout the Church reveal that LDS young people who remained steadfast, solid, and straight in the midst of serious temptation were those whose parents had helped them to internalize the gospel, to make personal scripture study and especially personal prayer high priorities in their lives. The following are some comments from active young Latter-day Saints who made it through challenges without losing their way, at least so far:

"I am so blessed now because my parents encouraged me to pray and read the scriptures on my own."

"My dad always reminds me, 'Say your prayers.' This reminds me that it is not enough to have family prayer. I must pray on my own."

"My parents taught me how important personal revelation is and how I could find answers in the scriptures and receive answers to my prayers."

"It was my parents' example that had the most effect on me. . . . They would give thoughts and advice, but they left it up to me. But they would always counsel me to turn to the Lord and find out his will. In doing this it helped me to start to have spiritual experiences in my own life." (Brent L. Top and Bruce A. Chadwick, *Rearing Righteous Youth of Zion* [Salt Lake City: Bookcraft, 1998], 89.)

These comments affirm the promise of President Ezra Taft Benson, who said to the youth, "If you will earnestly seek guidance from your Heavenly Father, morning and evening, you will be given the strength to shun any temptation." (In Conference Report, October 1977, 46.) We all know that such a promise applies equally to the rest of us.

> *Awake, ye Saints of God, awake!*
> *Call on the Lord in mighty prayer*
> *That he will Zion's bondage break*
> *And bring to naught the tempter's snare.*
>
> *Tho Zion's foes have counseled deep,*
> *Although they bind with fetters strong,*
> *The God of Jacob does not sleep;*
> *His vengeance will not slumber long.*
>
> *With constant faith and fervent prayer,*
> *With deep humility of soul,*
> *With steadfast mind and heart, prepare*
> *To see th' eternal purpose roll.*
>
> *Awake to righteousness; be one,*
> *Or, saith the Lord, "Ye are not mine!"*
> *Yea, like the Father and the Son,*
> *Let all the Saints in union join.*
>   ("Awake, Ye Saints of God, Awake!" *Hymns*, no. 17.)

There are prayers, and then there are prayers. Sometimes we need to pray with a light spirit and without heavy and deep need weighing upon us. At other times, we long for the kind of spiritual contact and association that demand our most strenuous and disciplined efforts. Jacob of old wrestled with an angel until the breaking of day and thus obtained a blessing from God. (Genesis 32:24–32.) Hungering and thirsting after righteousness, Enos wrestled with the Lord in prayer all day and into the night, until the holy voice declared that his sins were forgiven. (Enos 1:1–8.) Our Lord and Savior came to know something about prayer that he could not have known before his entrance into mortality. In the Garden of Gethsemane, the Savior began to feel the loss of his Father's sustaining Spirit. "And being in an agony," Luke records, "he prayed more earnestly." (Luke 22:44.) In writing of this singular occasion, Elder Bruce R. McConkie observed: "Now here is a marvelous thing. Note it well. The Son of God 'prayed more earnestly'! He who did all things well, whose every word was right, whose every emphasis was proper; he to whom the Father gave his Spirit without measure; he who was the only perfect being ever to walk the dusty paths of planet earth—the Son of God 'prayed more earnestly,' teaching us, his brethren [and sisters], that all prayers, his included, are not alike, and that a greater need calls forth more earnest and faith-filled pleadings before the throne of him to whom the prayers of the saints are a sweet savor." ("Why the Lord Ordained Prayer," in *Prayer* [Salt Lake City: Deseret Book 1977], 8.)

Indeed, some thorns in the flesh call forth prayers of great intensity (2 Corinthians 12:7–10), supplications and pleadings that are certainly out of the ordinary. Such vexations of the soul are not typical, not part of our daily prayer life. Just as it would be a mistake to suppose that Jacob or Enos wrestled with God in prayer every day, so you and I are not expected to involve ourselves with the same tenacity, to be involved in the same bending of the soul on a regular basis. But now and then, in the eternal scheme of things, we must pass through the fire to come through life purified and refined and thus prepared to dwell one day in everlasting burnings with God and Christ and other holy beings.

If we are willing to move beyond a casual relationship with God, willing to spend the time and exert the energy necessary to make of our prayer life something more than it is now, then great things await us. For one thing, in time and with experience, our prayers can become more than petitions, as important as it is to petition the Lord. Our prayers can become instructive, the means whereby God can reveal great and important things to us. The apostle Paul taught us that "the Spirit also helpeth our infirmities: for we know not what we should pray for as we ought: but the Spirit itself maketh intercession for us with [striving] which cannot be [expressed]." (Romans 8:26.) (Compare Joseph Smith, *Teachings of the Prophet Joseph Smith,* comp. Joseph Fielding Smith [Salt Lake City: Deseret Book, 1976], 278; 3 Nephi 19:24; D&C 46:30; 50:29–30; 63:65.) That is to say, if we are quiet and attentive, the Spirit of the Lord can, on some occasions, lead us to pray for things that were not on our personal agenda, things deep down, things that pertain more to our eternal needs than our temporal wants. At such times we find our words reaching beyond our thoughts, praying for people and circumstances and eventualities that surprise us.

"God sees things as they really are," Elder Neal A. Maxwell wrote, "and as they will become. We don't! In order to tap that precious perspective during our prayers, we must rely upon the promptings of the Holy Ghost. With access to that kind of knowledge, we would then pray for what we and others should have—really have. With the Spirit prompting us, we will not pray 'amiss.'

"With access to the Spirit, our circles of concern will expand.

The mighty prayer of Enos began with understandable self-concern, moved outward to family, then to his enemies, and then outward to future generations." ("What Should We Pray For?" in *Prayer* [Salt Lake City: Deseret Book, 1977], 45.)

We kneel before God to show our reverence toward him and where possible speak our prayers aloud, but many times in the day we are not able to kneel or give voice to our yearnings or our feelings. So it is that we have the commission to "pray always," to keep a prayer in our hearts, to speak to the Almighty in our mind. We pray for his direction and his strength in school, in our work, in our studies, in our athletic endeavors, and in counseling with troubled friends or confused loved ones. Amulek invites us to "cry unto him for mercy; for he is mighty to save. Yea, humble yourselves, and continue in prayer unto him. Cry unto him when ye are in your fields, yea, over all your flocks. Cry unto him in your houses, yea, over all your household, both morning, mid-day, and evening. Yea, cry unto him against the power of your enemies. Yea, cry unto him against the devil, who is an enemy to all righteousness. Cry unto him over the crops of your fields, that ye may prosper in them. Cry over the flocks of your fields, that they may increase. But this is not all; ye must pour out your souls in your closets, and your secret places, and in your wilderness. Yea, and when you do not cry unto the Lord, let your hearts be full, drawn out in prayer unto him continually for your welfare, and also for the welfare of those who are around you." (Alma 34:18–27.)

Alma also implored, "Cry unto God for all thy support; yea, let all thy doings be unto the Lord, and whithersoever thou goest let it be in the Lord; yea, let all thy thoughts be directed unto the Lord; yea, let the affections of thy heart be placed upon the Lord forever. Counsel with the Lord in all thy doings, and he will direct thee for good; yea, when thou liest down at night lie down unto the Lord, that he may watch over you in your sleep; and when thou risest in the morning let thy heart be full of thanks unto God; and if ye do these things, ye shall be lifted up at the last day." (Alma 37:36–37.)

As President Boyd K. Packer pointed out some years ago, the moral pollution index in our society is rising. (In Conference Report, April 1992, 91.) Evil is on the loose. "Satan is abroad in the land" (D&C 52:14); it is truly the day of his power. We cannot resist the incessant pull of immorality nor escape the desensitization that follows naturally from larger doses of harshness, crudeness, and violence without the infusion of spiritual power that comes through communion with the Infinite. Not one of us is invulnerable to satanic influences. Not one of us is strong enough to confront the enemy alone.

I know that prayer makes available that balm of Gilead that comes to us from God in heaven through his Holy Spirit. Peace and perspective come to us as we come unto him. I know that God our Father lives, that he knows us and hears our prayers. When we pray, we are speaking not to a force in the universe but to the Father of our spirits. I know that we can refine and purify our lives through a greater attention to the regularity, intensity, and overall quality of our prayers. That we will more consistently pour out our souls in prayer as individuals and as families that the Lord may pour out upon us a blessing hitherto unknown, is the earnest desire of my heart.

The Power
of Prayer

PRESIDENT N. ELDON TANNER

I HAVE GREAT FAITH in prayer. I constantly pray that those who doubt might be helped to see and understand that God is our Father, that we are his spirit children, that he is really there and has said, "Ask, and it shall be given you; seek, and ye shall find; knock, and it shall be opened unto you: For every one that asketh receiveth; and he that seeketh findeth; and to him that knocketh it shall be opened." (Matthew 7:7–8.)

I often wonder if we really realize the power of prayer, if we appreciate what a great blessing it is to be able to call on our Father in heaven in humble prayer, knowing that he is interested in us and that he wants us to succeed.

As the late Elder Richard L. Evans so beautifully said: "Our Father in heaven is not an umpire who is trying to count us out. He is not a competitor who is trying to outsmart us. He is not a prosecutor who is trying to convict us. He is a loving Father who wants our happiness and eternal progress and who will help us all he can if we will but give him in our lives an opportunity to do so with obedience and humility, and faith and patience." (Conference Report, Oct. 1956, 101.)

To pray effectively, and to feel that one can be heard and have his prayers answered, one must believe that he is praying to a God who can hear and answer, one who is interested in his children and their well-being. The first record we have of anyone praying to the Lord is that recorded by Moses in these words. "And Adam and Eve, his wife, called upon the name of the Lord, and they heard the voice of the Lord from the way toward the Garden of Eden, speaking unto them, and they saw him not; . . . And Adam and Eve, his wife, ceased not to call upon God." (Moses 5:4, 16.)

Great and influential men have always prayed for divine guidance. Even this great nation was founded on prayer. U.S. Senator Strom Thurmond of South Carolina reminded us of this when he said:

"The Mayflower Compact, written in November of 1620, begins with a prayer, 'In the name of God,' and goes on to state: 'We . . . having undertaken, for the glory of God, . . . do by these presents solemnly and mutually in the presence of God, and of one another, covenant and combine ourselves together into a civil body politic.'

"Thus our nation began founded on prayer. The kneeling figure of George Washington through that bitter winter in Valley Forge is a part of this country that should never be forgotten. . . .

"The Constitutional Convention in June of 1787 had been meeting for weeks without agreement, when Benjamin Franklin rose to his feet and addressed George Washington:

"'Mr. President: The small progress we have made after four or five weeks close attention and continual reasonings with each other . . . is a melancholy proof of the imperfection of the human understanding. . . . We have gone back to ancient history for models of government that now no longer exist. And we have viewed modern states . . . but find none of their constitutions suitable to our circumstances. . . . How has it happened, Sir, that we have not, hitherto, once thought of humbly applying to the Father of Light to illuminate our understandings?

"'In the beginning of the contest with Britain, when we were sensible of danger, we had daily prayers in this room for divine protection.

"'Our prayers, Sir, were heard; and they were generously answered. . . .

"'I, therefore, beg leave to move:—

"'That henceforth, prayers imploring the assistance of Heaven and its blessings on our deliberations be held in this assembly every morning before we proceed to business.'" ("A Priceless Asset," *Spotlight,* May 1966.)

This was done, and now we enjoy the fruits of their labors in answer to prayer. Prayer has never been outmoded in this great country. Abraham Lincoln, who prayed to the Lord continually for guidance, said: "It is the duty of nations as well as of men to own their dependence upon the overruling power of God, to confess their sins and transgressions in humble sorrow . . . and to recognize the sublime truth that those nations only are blessed whose God is the Lord."

President Dwight D. Eisenhower, at the time of his inauguration, petitioned the Lord: "Give us, we pray, the power to discern clearly right from wrong, and to allow all our works and actions to be governed thereby, and by the laws of this land . . . so that all may work for the good of our beloved country, and for thy glory. Amen."

Samuel F. B. Morse, inventor of the telegraph, said that

whenever he could not see his way clearly, he knelt down and prayed for light and understanding.

We have that sweet and simple prayer recorded by astronaut Gordon Cooper while orbiting the earth: "Father, thank you, especially for letting me fly this flight. Thank you for the privilege of being able to be in this position, to be up in this wondrous place, seeing all these many startling, wonderful things that you have created."

I join with Senator Thurmond in his appeal to our people "to pray more, to examine the religious heritage of our country, and to see the benefit of seeking God's blessings. Prayer is the only way in which the finite can communicate with the infinite; . . . in which the visible may be in touch with the invisible. You may easily see, if you but examine the history of our Nation, that prayer and communication with God is the very cornerstone of our society. If you allow it to be abandoned now, you will be casting away the greatest asset this Nation, or any other nation, has ever known."

All of the prophets, from Adam to our present prophet, have prayed unceasingly for guidance, and even the Savior prayed continually to God the Eternal Father. We read, regarding the Savior: "And it came to pass in those days, that he went out into a mountain to pray, and continued all night in prayer to God." (Luke 6:12.)

The Lord has admonished all of us to pray, and through the prophet James has given us this promise: "If any of you lack wisdom, let him ask of God, that giveth to all men liberally, and upbraideth not; and it shall be given him. But let him ask in faith, nothing wavering. For he that wavereth is like a wave of the sea driven with the wind and tossed." (James 1:5–6.)

This promise is given to every one of us—high and low, rich and poor. It is universal, unrestricted to you and to me and to our neighbors. He has told us that we must believe and have faith in God. We should know that the Lord stands ready to help his children if they will put themselves in tune through prayer and by keeping his commandments. In fact, the Lord has said: "I, the Lord, am bound when ye do what I say; but when ye do not what I say, ye have no promise." (D&C 82:10.)

We must be prepared to recognize that God is the Creator of the world, and that he, through his Son Jesus Christ and his prophets, has given us in simple language information regarding man's relationship to God, our pre-earth existence, the purpose of our mission here on earth, and the fact that our postmortal existence, or our life after death, is real, and that what we do here will condition us for the world to come.

We must not be misled by the doctrines of men. All the studies of science and philosophy will never answer this question: "What is man and why is he here?" But it is answered clearly and simply in the gospel of Jesus Christ, and we are instructed: "If any of you lack wisdom, let him ask of God." (James 1:5.)

Let us be prepared to do this and not be as those to whom the Savior referred, when he said: "Well did Esaias prophesy of you, saying, This people draweth nigh unto me with their mouth, and honoureth me with their lips; but their heart is far from me. But in vain they do worship me, teaching for doctrines the commandments of men." (Matthew 15:7–9.)

Yes, it is important, and the Lord emphasizes that we must humble ourselves and accept the teachings of Jesus Christ and keep his commandments if we would expect him to hear and answer our prayers. We should all be prepared to say truthfully, as Paul did, in speaking to the Romans, "For I am not ashamed of the gospel of Christ: for it is the power of God unto salvation to every one that believeth." (Romans 1:16.)

It is difficult to understand why some cannot believe, or find it very hard to believe that God can hear and answer our prayers, and yet they believe that astronauts can leave the earth and travel in outer space at thousands of miles per hour and still be directed from home base; that they can keep in touch with home base and receive instructions and be led in their activities and then be brought back to a safe landing here upon the earth.

How can we question God's ability to hear and answer our prayers and direct us in all things if we will but keep in tune with him, and at the same time have no doubt that marvelous machines and men can be sent out from the earth to the moon and there be directed by mere man here upon the earth?

We are as astronauts, sent out by God to fill our missions here upon the earth. He wants us to succeed. He stands ready to answer our prayers and assures us a safe landing as we return if we will but keep in touch with him through prayer and do as we are bid.

As we pray, however, are we prepared to ask the Lord to bless us as we answer his call or acknowledge and serve him?

Are we prepared to ask the Lord to forgive us as we forgive one another?

We may well stop and analyze our own situation. Do we wait until we are in trouble and then run to the Lord? As we pray, do we give orders to the Lord by saying, "Bless this," and "Bless that," "Give us this," and "Give us that," "Do this," and "Do that"?

Or do we pray that we might be led to do that which is right, or be blessed with those things which are for our best good? We should always pray for the desire and strength and determination to do the will of our Heavenly Father, and always stand ready to do his bidding.

Men pray for different reasons. Many are driven to their knees out of fear, and then only do they pray. Others go to the Lord when in dire need of immediate direction for which they know of no other place to go. Nations are called by their governments in case of a national tragedy, drought, or plague, famine or war, to call upon God for his blessings, for his protection, and for his direction. Some people ask to be healed, others to be strengthened. They ask for the blessings of the Lord to attend their families, their loved ones, and themselves in all their righteous endeavors. This, I am sure, is all good in the sight of the Lord.

It is most important, however, that we take time to express our gratitude to our Father in heaven for the many blessings we receive.

As we express our appreciation for our many blessings, we become more conscious of what the Lord has done for us, and thereby we become more appreciative. We all know what it means to hear or receive an expression of gratitude for anything we might have done. Our forefathers set aside a day of thanksgiving. I fear that some of us even forget that day.

I wonder if we are sometimes guilty of not expressing to the Lord our gratitude, even as the lepers who were healed. We all remember so well the story of Jesus healing the ten lepers, who cried:

"Have mercy on us.

"And one of them, when he saw that he was healed, turned back, and with a loud voice glorified God,

"And fell down on his face at his feet, giving him thanks: and he was a Samaritan.

"And Jesus answering said, Were there not ten cleansed? but where are the nine?

"There are not found that returned to give glory to God, save this stranger." (Luke 17:13, 15–18.)

And as Mark Antony said when referring to Caesar, who recognized his friend Brutus among his assassins,

This was the most unkindest cut of all;
For when the noble Caesar saw him stab,
Ingratitude, more strong than traitors' arms,
Quite vanquished him: then burst his mighty heart.
(Julius Caesar, Act 3, sc. 2)

I am sure that the Lord expects us to express our gratitude for our many blessings as we ask for his continued blessings, and to ask forgiveness for our failings and the desire and strength to do right.

When we pray, it is important that we set about to do all in our power to make it possible for the Lord to answer our prayers. As my father said to me when I was just a boy, "My son, if you want your prayers to be answered, you must get on your feet and do your part."

I often think how much more effective it would be, when the country's president calls upon his people to set aside a day of prayer, if we were all living righteous lives and were prepared to acknowledge God as our Creator and keep his commandments. It seems that many have lost belief in God entirely, and many question his ability to answer our prayers. Others have faith and confidence in their own learning and in their own strength and power.

The Lord has instructed parents to teach their children to have faith in Christ, the Son of the living God, and to pray and to walk uprightly before the Lord. There is no doubt that our children, if they are taught to pray to a living God in whom they have faith, can more easily walk uprightly before the Lord.

I shall never be able to express fully my appreciation to my parents for teaching me to pray secretly and to participate with them in family prayer. My mother taught me at her knee. She made me feel and know that I was talking to the Lord, to our Maker, our Father in heaven, and that he was conscious of my acts and my wishes and my needs. I was taught that I should express my sincere thanks, ask for forgiveness, and ask for strength to do the right. This has always been a great strength to me throughout my life, and today I pray even more diligently than I ever did before that the Lord will guide and direct me in my activities, that whatever I do will be acceptable to him.

As I think back to when we used to kneel as a family in prayer every morning and every evening, I realize what it meant to us as children to hear our father call upon the Lord and actually talk to him, expressing his gratitude and asking for the blessings of the Lord on his crops and flocks and all of our undertakings. It always gave us greater strength to meet temptation when we remembered that we would be reporting to the Lord at night.

Family prayer in any home will draw the family closer together and result in better feelings between father and mother, between parents and children, and between one child and another. If children pray for their parents, it makes them more appreciative of their parents, and as they pray for one another, they feel closer to one another and part of each other, especially as they realize that they are talking to their Father in heaven while on their knees in family or secret prayer. Then is when we forget our differences and think of the best in others, and pray for their well-being and for strength to overcome our own weaknesses. There is no doubt that we are better people when we try to tune in to the spirit of our Father in heaven so that we might communicate with him and express our desire to do his will as we pray for his blessings.

The Lord has admonished us to "pray always, lest you enter into temptation and lose your reward. Be faithful unto the end, and lo, I am with you. These words are not of man nor of men, but of me, even Jesus Christ, your Redeemer, by the will of the Father." (D&C 31:12–13.)

I have often asked myself and tried to answer this question: Why do some people refuse to pray? Is it because they feel they have not the time?

I remember very well a father coming to me one day regarding his oldest son, with whom he was having some difficulty. The boy was a good boy, but he was getting out of hand. I asked the father if they had regular family prayers in their home. He answered, "Well, no, but sometimes. You know, we are too busy and we go to work at different times, and therefore it is most difficult for our family to get together for family prayer."

I asked, "If you knew that your boy was sick nigh unto death, would you be able to get your family together each night and morning for a week to pray that his life might be spared?"

"Why, of course," he said.

I tried then to explain to him that there are other ways of losing a boy than by death. I also explained that when families pray together, they usually stay together, and their ideals are higher, they feel more secure, and they have a greater love for one another.

Do people not pray because they feel too independent, too smart, and think they can go it alone? Or are they ashamed to call upon God? Do they think it shows a weakness? Or do they not believe in or have faith in God? Or is it that they do not appreciate their many blessings? Or do they not feel worthy? If one does not feel worthy, he should acknowledge his weaknesses, express regret, repent, covenant to do right, and ask for guidance.

Is it because some do not know how to pray? If that is true, I suggest that you go to your Heavenly Father in secret. Pour out your heart to him. Pray regularly so that you can feel at home and comfortable while communicating with him. All one needs to do is express his feelings, which the Lord understands. He has invited all of us to call on him regularly and has promised that he will hear our supplication.

The ancient prophet Moroni, referring to the Book of Mormon, said:

"And when ye shall receive these things, I would exhort you that ye would ask God, the Eternal Father, in the name of Christ, if these things are not true; and if ye shall ask with a sincere heart, with real intent, having faith in Christ, he will manifest the truth of it unto you, by the power of the Holy Ghost.

"And by the power of the Holy Ghost ye may know the truth of all things." (Moroni 10:4–5.)

This promise applies to all of us if we will but repent and go to the Lord, knowing that he can hear and will hear and answer our prayers. We should all realize that we are God's children and that he is still as interested in us as he ever was. He still answers the prayers of the righteous and those who diligently seek him.

Keeping
in Touch

A R D E T H   G R E E N E   K A P P

HELLO! HELLO! I'm sorry I can't hear you!" I shouted into the telephone. Hanging up the phone, I searched anxiously for another one somewhere away from the noise and commotion of the people from many lands, speaking different languages, going in every direction, at the Heathrow Airport in London, England. That tower of Babel incident really caused a problem, I thought, as I observed one traveler unsuccessfully seeking information in a language foreign to another, followed by a gesture they both could translate: a shrug of the shoulders meaning, "I don't understand." They could hear each other all right, but it was obvious the message was not getting through.

Mine was a different problem. I couldn't hear. Trying to hold back the tears and feeling so far away from home, I located another telephone down the concourse. I had been in the British Isles on an assignment for over three weeks. I had planned to take the train from Stoke-on-Trent to London for my 4:15 P.M. flight to Los Angeles. If I could just get that far, I thought, I could even walk the rest of the way to Utah if necessary. Due to a difference in the train schedules from weekday to Sunday, however, I missed my connection for the 4:15 flight by twenty minutes. The plane headed for home was in the air, but I was on the ground. I needed to call home. I wanted to be home. An emptiness crowded in, and I felt sick—homesick.

Locating another telephone, I read the instructions carefully, then once again dialed the international number printed on my telephone credit card. First a number, followed by the letter M, then three more numbers grouped together, plus three more, then four numbers, and finally the number eight. Twelve numbers in all, plus the letter M. I waited anxiously, hoping for a clear connection as I heard the call going through. How does this magic of communication across continents, under the ocean, in outer space, take place?

In my state of homesickness, I returned in my mind to my home when I was a child. I could see the calendar on the wall with our telephone number clearly printed at the bottom. My mother owned and operated a little country store, and each year she gave her customers and friends a calendar with a different picture for each season. But the information printed on the bottom was always the same. It could hardly be considered advertising since there was no competitor, but the information was important and seemed to lend prestige to our small business. It read in black letters:

Greene's General Store
Groceries, Dry Goods, Novelties
Glenwood, Alberta, Phone #3.

I didn't need a telephone calling card to remember #3.

The phone, like a large box, hung on the wall with a silver-colored receiver you held to your ear. We could pick up the receiver almost any time of the day and hear any one of ten people whom we knew and loved exchanging valuable information. A party line, we called it. Sister Woodruff would be giving a recipe for baked beans or some other dish to Sister Glines, who missed Relief Society the week when the recipe was shared. And if you didn't get in on the beginning of the conversation, it was never a problem for Sister Woodruff to repeat it. Communication was wonderful in those days until after six o'clock, when the switchboard, located in my grandmother's house, was closed for the day and the operator did not come on duty again until eight o'clock the following morning. In the case of an emergency, a loud siren-like sound could be heard anywhere in the house and would bring someone running to take the call.

Surely this was an emergency, I thought as I waited in the phone booth in London. Someone will answer. I anxiously waited as the telephone rang six, seven, eight times. Oh, if I could just get through to one of those old-time operators of long ago who answered "Information please" with such feeling and concern, I knew I'd feel better. She could always report on where you might locate any person in the town, what they were doing, and when they might be home if they didn't answer their phone.

Our operator could always answer our questions and was the source of all the important information for our little village. Someone who was going to Cardston and had room for an extra passenger in the car would call Operator and leave word. On the other hand, anyone who needed a ride to Cardston and did not have a way would also call Operator. She was the source of all the information that kept our town connected. On some occasions, information flowed so freely there were more connections than you might want. But that's the way with a small town, and we wouldn't have changed it.

The twentieth century has brought with it unbelievable technology, providing communication through the most sophisticated procedures. It has been described as a period of time that has taken us from "muttering machines to laser beams." With all of the advancement that has been made, for many, however, the communication lines remain down with no connection. Not across the ocean or the continent, but across the room, across the table, in our own homes. There are times for many when no one calls and no one answers; and if they do, it is like foreigners at Heathrow Airport—a shrug of the shoulders meaning, "I don't understand you. It doesn't make sense to me. I can hear you, but your message is not getting through."

Some time ago, a young woman traveling from one distant state to another stopped in Salt Lake City. She was en route to her grandmother's home, where she was planning to live for a while. I met her when she visited my office, having called in advance for an appointment. She was an attractive young woman about sixteen years of age. We sat together on the couch in my office, and through the west window, we could see the Salt Lake Temple. She was obviously nervous. At first she responded only to my questions, as I attempted to become acquainted with her. Getting nowhere at all, I finally asked Jennifer (not her real name), "How are things with you at home? Tell me about your family, your brothers and sisters, your parents."

There was silence. She fidgeted with something in her hands, then shook her head and whispered, "It's not good, not good at all." I waited for her to explain further. "You see," she said, tears filling her eyes, "my mom won't ever talk to me, and she won't listen." Biting her lower lip to control her tears, she continued, "She listens to others but not to me. I'm the youngest one in our family, and my mom won't ever listen to me."

"That must be hard," I responded quietly.

"Yes," she said, "because I love my mom. Why won't she talk to me?" she sobbed. "I'm going to live with my grandmother for a while because Mom and I just can't get along."

"Don't get along?"

"Yes, we don't ever talk to each other. It's so hard . . . because"—she hesitated and wiped her eyes—"because I love her."

"Have you ever told her so?" I asked. She shook her head. "Do you think she would like to know? Could you write your feelings and express your love for her in a letter?"

"Maybe."

"Will you?" I asked. She agreed she would. "Would you like to get a letter of love from your mom? And if you did, would you bother to read it?" I asked.

"Yes, oh yes," she whispered.

"And would you answer?"

She nodded.

After listening to Jennifer for some time and allowing her to discuss her concerns, I asked if it would be acceptable with her if I were to call her mother and tell her that we had talked and that she had expressed love for her mother. Without hesitation she agreed, and she gave me the area code and the telephone number for her parents' home.

As Jennifer left my office, I gave her a warm hug and expressed my love. "Thanks, thanks for listening," she said. "I'll write to my mom."

I watched her as she waited at the elevator. The doors opened, and she got in and waved good-bye. Then the doors closed, and she was gone. Returning to my desk, I asked over and over in my mind, *What kind of a mother must this beautiful and sensitive young woman have?* I would find out. I dialed the number she had given me.

"Hello," a cheery voice answered. I identified myself and then verified that I was speaking to Jennifer's mother. She certainly sounded pleasant enough, although a bit surprised that I would be calling her.

"I'm calling," I explained, "to tell you of my visit with your daughter."

"Really?"

"I've enjoyed visiting with your daughter. I'm impressed with her," I said. "She tells me she is going to live with her grand-mother."

"Yes," her mother responded. "It seems like it might be better that way. But it's very hard." Her voice filled with emotion. "You see, Sister Kapp, the problem is, Jenny won't ever talk to me, and she just won't listen. We can't communicate." Like an echo from a familiar phrase, I heard again, "She won't talk to me, and she won't listen." The woman hesitated, then explained, "I love her so much, but a barrier, like a wall, has grown up between us, and it seems like I can't get through to her."

We talked for some time. I told her of the love her daughter had expressed for her. "I think she would like to get a letter from you," I said, "and maybe you could write about your tender feelings for her."

"I will. I will today," she promised.

Many times since that conversation the familiar phrase plays on the memory of my mind, "She won't talk to me, and she won't listen." I hear the hurt in Jennifer's voice and the anxiety in her mother's. The lines were down. There was no operator to help get the message through, and the distance between them was increasing.

We are all away from home in the sense that we cannot talk to our Father in heaven face to face, and we long to call home, but many times it seems that we can't get through. The fact is that a veil separates us from our heavenly home for a time, but that need never ever keep us from communicating, talking, listening, being in touch, expressing love, and feeling the love our Father has for us. There are times when we may feel far away from home and out of touch, when we've missed our plane connection, so to speak, and the lines are temporarily down. We begin to yearn for that close contact with home, yet feel so far away. We may think, *My Father doesn't talk to me and he doesn't listen. My prayers don't get through.*

And what of the times when we struggle up steep and rocky slopes in times of trials and tests? Is it possible our Father watches tenderly and is willing and anxious to give help and comfort, guidance and warnings, but he can't get through to us because we don't talk to him, and we don't listen even though we have been warned?

"Behold, verily, verily, I say unto you, ye must watch and pray always lest ye enter into temptation; for Satan desireth to have you, that he may sift you as wheat," Jesus taught the Nephites. "Therefore ye must always pray unto the Father in my name." (3 Nephi 18:18–19.)

Too often we fail to ask and we do not listen with full anticipation of receiving an answer. Maybe we really don't even expect an answer.

For some time I have had a little sign on my file cabinet at home that was given to me at a Young Women conference. It says simply, "Remember, you are a child of God. Call home." I've often pondered that simple admonition. What does it mean to call home?

Would I use number three as I did as a child, or the international number of twelve digits that I used in the airport? Is there an area code that must precede the number for me to get through in prayer? And is there a charge? Would I get a bill, and how much might it be? How long could I talk?

Nephi understood how to talk and listen to the Lord. He explained, "I . . . did go into the mount oft, and I did pray oft unto the Lord; wherefore the Lord showed unto me great things." (1 Nephi 18:3.)

First we must desire to talk to our Heavenly Father and to listen to him, knowing that he in turn will talk to us in our minds and in our hearts (D&C 8:2) and will listen to us. There is no question about his promise to us. He has said, "Draw near unto me and I will draw near unto you; seek me diligently and ye shall find me; ask, and ye shall receive; knock, and it shall be opened unto you. Whatsoever ye ask the Father in my name it shall be given unto you, that is expedient for you." (D&C 88:63–64.)

In time and when our hearts are full and we know not that for which we should pray, the Spirit will make intercession for us even without the words. (See Romans 8:26.) Our feelings, our desires are heard through our prayers.

"If ye would hearken unto the Spirit which teacheth a man to pray ye would know that ye must pray; for the evil spirit teacheth not a man to pray, but teacheth him that he must not pray. But behold, I say unto you that ye must pray always, and not faint; that ye must not perform any thing unto the Lord save in the first place ye shall pray unto the Father in the name of Christ, that he will consecrate thy performance unto thee, that thy performance may be for the welfare of thy soul." (2 Nephi 32:8–9.)

The scriptures become personal messages to us when we liken them unto ourselves. (1 Nephi 19:23.) Our Savior becomes our advocate and prays to the Father in our behalf, even pleading our cause. He has said, "Wherefore, Father, spare these my brethren [and we can put our own name here] that believe on my name, that they may come unto me and have everlasting life." (D&C 45:5.)

God is our Father. We are his children. We were together in his presence at one time. Jesus, our elder Brother, has made possible an eternal family relationship when we do our part. Think of it! When we understand that relationship, our prayers become natural and instinctive, personal and very real. If we don't remember this relationship between us and our Father, we experience difficulties with prayer. Our prayers become routine and mechanical.

In the Bible Dictionary we read: "Prayer is the act by which the will of the Father and the will of the child are brought into correspondence with each other. The object of prayer is not to change the will of God, but to secure for ourselves and for others blessings that God is already willing to grant, but that are made conditional on our asking for them. Blessings require some work or effort on our part before we can obtain them. Prayer is a form of work, and is an appointed means for obtaining the highest of all blessings." (LDS Edition of the King James Version, 1979, 752–53 of Appendix.)

This form of work requires some important preparation on our part if it is to be effective. In a talk to Church Education teachers in 1956, President Harold B. Lee, who was then a member of the Council of the Twelve, talked about a lesson he had learned from President David O. McKay: "The President made the statement that . . . when we are relaxed in a private room, we are more susceptible [to the promptings of the Spirit]; and that so far as he is concerned, his best thoughts come after he gets up in the morning and is relaxed and thinking about the duties of the day; that impressions come more clearly, as if it were a voice." Then President

Lee commented, "Those impressions are right. If we are worried about something and upset in our feelings, the inspiration does not come. If we so live that our minds are free from worry and our conscience is clear and our feelings are right toward one another, the operation of the Spirit of the Lord upon our spirit is as real as when we pick up the telephone; but when they come, we must be brave enough to take the suggested actions." (Talk to seminary and institute of religion teachers, July 6, 1956.)

We learn to talk and we learn to listen, and often while reading the scriptures, we will hear the voice of the Lord in our mind and in our heart by the promptings of the Holy Ghost. (D&C 8:2.) We come to know the Lord's will concerning us as we ponder the direction given in our patriarchal blessings when he speaks to us in a very personal way through his appointed servant, the patriarch.

You will remember the story of Hannah, who prayed for a son and vowed to give him to the Lord. Then Samuel was born, and as a youth he went to live with Eli the priest. One night he had a very personal experience. The Lord called him, and the young boy, thinking it was Eli, ran to Eli and responded, "Here am I. Did you call me?"

Eli explained that he had not called him and counseled the child to lie down again and go back to sleep. The Lord called again. Samuel arose and went to Eli and repeated, "Here am I." Eli responded, "I called not, my son; lie down again."

The Lord called a third time, and Samuel once again said, "Here am I, for thou didst call me." This time Eli perceived that the Lord had called the child, and he counseled him that if he were called again, he was to say, "Speak, Lord; for thy servant heareth."

Once again the Lord called, "Samuel, Samuel." This time Samuel answered, "Speak; for thy servant heareth." (1 Samuel 3:1–10.)

Our Father talks to us as surely as he spoke to Samuel, although perhaps not in the same way, and he listens. We can talk to him and we can listen. When we do, we are never far from home. Our call home allows us to talk as long as we want and to listen as long as we will. The price we pay is simply to always remember him and keep his commandments so that we can have his Spirit with us always.

Index

Aaron, 53

Abraham, 107

Accountability, 44

Adam: fall of, 2, 134; commanded to pray, 6, 16, 37; heard voice of Lord, 159

Adoration, 27

Agency, 11–12, 13–14, 82, 134

Airport, story about, 169–71

Alma the Elder, prayed for son, 18, 45

Alma the Younger: father prayed for, 18, 45; counseled Helaman, 37; on prayer, 46, 156

Amulek, 8, 10, 13, 39

Answers: require work, 11, 88, 139–41, 165; to every prayer, 18–20, 42–46, 125, 137; are for our good, 21–23, 135–36; and the Spirit, 31, 98–99; different kinds of, 40; how to receive, 46, 70, 131, 177–78; "no," 46, 136–37, 141; accepting, 62–63, 102; recognizing, 100; come through friends, 101

Atonement, 1–5

"Awake, Ye Saints of God, Awake!" 153

Baptism, 60

Beecher, Henry Ward, 46, 147

Benson, Ezra Taft, 75, 153

Bitter cup, 4, 28, 46

Bitterness, 44

Blessings: follow prayer, 6–7, 8–9, 125; require work, 37; counting, 50–51, 104–6; thanking God for, 65–66; priesthood, 102; tribulation follows, 106

Book of Mormon, 20, 87–88, 96

Bosom, burning in, 88

Bread, daily, 27–28

Brown, Hugh B., 102

Caesar, 165

Callings, 28, 71

Childbirth, 106–8, 119–20

Children: prayers of, 19–20, 118; wanting more, 101–2; praying for, 102–3; protecting, 112; peace of, 113; faith of, 113–14; teaching, to pray, 117–25, 165–66

Clark, J. Reuben, 60–61

Closet, praying in, 95, 113, 130, 156

Communication: prayer as, 5–6, 13; opening path of, 36; desire for, 135–37; in families, 172–75

Communion, with God: prayer unlocks door to, 20, 24, 110; barriers to, 146; feeling comfortable with, 147, 167–68

Confidence, 89

Conscience, 30–31, 70, 178

Constitution, 159–60

Cooper, Gordon, 161

Covenants, 64, 91

Cowdery, Oliver, 18–19, 87–88

Craven, Rulon G., 99

Crises, 126

Crucifixion, 52

Daniel, 27, 64

Dating, 98–100

Death, 52, 106–7

Decisions, 11–12, 29

Desires, 22, 29, 53, 87

Disobedience, 82, 124

Dissertation, story about, 138

Distraction, 146

Doubt, 51

Drought, 103

Edmunds, Mary Ellen, 32

Eisenhower, Dwight D., 160

Eli, 178

Enemies, praying for, 27, 50

Energy, praying with, 93–110, 120, 124–25, 154

England, story of missionaries in, 78–79

Enoch, 115–16

Enos: received forgiveness, 18; prayed for self, 23; prayed for hours, 30, 46–47, 105, 154; was prepared for prayer, 86–87, 154

Evans, Richard L., 39, 158–59

Eve: commanded to pray, 6, 16, 37; fall of, 134; heard voice of Lord, 159

Example, 117, 125

Faith: walking by, 5, 11, 16; prayers without, 26; asking in, 51, 87; lack of, 82; in Christ, 89; to accept Father's

will, 106; for healing, 108; in children, 113, 121; that God will answer, 159, 165

Fall, the, 134

False doctrine, 7

Family: praying for, 9, 26, 52, 102, 119; discussing prayer with, 91; and society, 111–12; as God's plan, 112; home evening, 112; as most important unit, 117; problems in, 172–75

Family prayer: Christ commanded that we have, 10, 17; importance of, 52, 118; Joseph Smith held, 63–64; memories of, 94; Spencer W. Kimball on, 111–16; making time for, 166–67

Farmers, story of two, 71

Fasting, 70, 78, 91

Fathers, 111

Fatigue, 30, 148

Fear, 80, 114, 163

Featherstone, Vaughn J., 117

Feelings, 53

Fields and flocks, 17, 28

First Vision, 58

Forgiveness: Enos received, 18; Joseph Smith prayed for, 26–27, 58; praying for, 28, 46–47, 77, 90; giving, to others, 77, 90, 94

Franklin, Benjamin, 159–60

Friends, answers come through, 101

Garden of Eden, 15–16

General Authorities, 26

Gethsemane, Christ's prayer in, 1–5, 9, 31, 46, 52, 154; earnestness of, 5, 154; included others, 9; gave Him strength, 31; got a "no" answer, 46, 136–37; remembering, 52

God the Father: and Gethsemane, 1–5; presence of, 5; addressing prayers to, 5–6, 7–8, 10; as one with Jesus Christ, 7–8; striving to be like, 15; kingdom of, 17–18; conforming to will of, 22, 24, 36, 99; praying that will of, be done, 28, 43, 102, 106–8, 127–28, 137–39, 163; sees reality, 23, 155; knows past, present, and future, 24, 44, 137–38; answers prayers, 35, 43,

98–99, 125, 135; relationship with, 36, 83, 133–34, 157, 175, 177; love of, 44, 48; listens to prayers, 48, 56, 162, 176; understands intentions, 56; confessing hand of, 76; desires our joy, 82, 144, 158–59; helps prepare us for prayer, 86; as source of power, 92, 129, 145; allows adversity, 127; losing contact with, 129, 175; wants us to pray, 130; wants us to return, 134, 163; knows us, 135, 141, 144; association with, 145
Groanings, 66–67, 84, 86, 97, 139

Habit, 84–85
Hamlet, 150
Hanks, Marion D., 82
Hannah, 178
Happiness, 35, 82, 92, 130
Harris, Martin, 29, 35, 63
Haun's Mill, 141–42
Healing, 107–8, 142
Heart: broken, 53, 88, 95; intents of, 56, 70, 86; prayer in, 76, 156; preparing, 88–89; yielding, 89; energy of, 93–110; change of, 104
Helaman, 127
Holland, Patricia, 38–39
Holy Ghost: praying for companionship of, 9; praying by power of, 11, 22–23, 78, 97; gives perspective, 23, 155; Joseph Smith on, 68–69; daily guidance of, 97. *See also* Spirit
Homesickness, 170, 175
Hosanna Shout, 68, 69
Humility, 63–64, 77, 94
Hunger, 86–87, 154
Hunter, Howard W., 147–48
Hunter, Oscar, 96
Hymns, 49, 100–101
Hypocrisy, 13, 30, 40

Independence, 167
Instruments, in God's hands, 40, 109
Intercessory prayer, 1–5, 9, 31, 46, 52, 154
Investigators, 9–10
Isaiah, 96, 109, 113

Jack, Elaine, 51
Jacob, 154
James, 8, 9, 147, 161
Jared, brother of, 16–17, 47
Jesus Christ: in Gethsemane, 1–5, 9, 31, 46, 52, 154; powers of, 3; disciples of, 3, 26, 28; prayed with Nephites, 4; resurrection of, 4; blood of, 4–5; earnestness in prayers of, 5, 25, 154; praying in name of, 7, 52, 151; answers prayers, 7–8; as one with God, 7–8; and the Lord's Prayer, 8, 27–28, 118, 138; perfection of, 15; on prayers being answered, 21; mind of, 22; ascension of, 28; high priestly prayer of, 28; stewardship of, 28; received "no" answer, 46, 136–37; crucifixion of, 52; second coming of, 61–62; Joseph Smith's vision of, 72–73; compassion of, 73; being like, 82, 110, 137; gratitude for, 105; invitation of, to come, 106; children of, 110; suffering of, 128; did Father's will, 137; and ten lepers, 164; as advocate, 176–77
Job, 86
Johnson, Father, 69

Kapp, Ardeth Greene, 169
Kimball, Spencer W.: on "no" answers, 46; on prayer as work, 46–47; and fasting, 103; taught by example, 125; trials of, 128; on making effort to receive answer, 140
King Benjamin, 42, 90, 147
Kingdom(s): of God, 17, 18; of glory, 82–83
Kirtland Temple, 60, 67
Knowledge, 8–9, 23, 24

Laman, 45
Lamoni, 53
Languages, 169–70
Leaders, 26, 50
Learning: to pray, 23, 29–31, 53–56, 130; from prayer, 24, 29, 61, 155; of Joseph Smith, 67
Lee, Harold B., 117, 123, 177

Lehi, 45, 91

Lepers, ten, 164

Lightner, Mary Elizabeth Rollins, 59

Lincoln, Abraham, 160

Listening: praying without, 48–49; with the Spirit, 61, 68; after praying, 78; and expecting an answer, 175; and Samuel, 178–79

Lombardi, Vince, 148

Lord's Prayer, the, 8, 27–28, 118, 138

Love: of God for us, 44, 48; praying to have more, 94, 110; fortifies, 106

Lyman, Francis M., 150

Madsen, Ann N., 93

Madsen, Truman G., 57

Magic wand, 40–42

Maxwell, Neal A., 21, 155–56

McConkie, Bruce R., 1, 46, 154

McKay, David O., 43, 117, 144, 177

Meditation, 91

Micah, 109

Millet, Robert L., 144

Miracles, 35, 43, 44, 142

Missionary work, 53–56, 78–79

Mormon, 11, 26, 110

Moroni: promise of, 20, 88, 96–97, 168; on charity, 110

Morse, Samuel F. B., 160–61

Mortality: as test, 11, 99; prayer as anchor in, 13; challenges in, 126–27; and veil, 134; importance of, 162

Moses, 25, 159

Moyle, Henry D., 71–72

Music, 92

Nature, 92

Nephi: on praying always, 8; on not asking amiss, 22; on Spirit teaching to pray, 35, 149; laments his sins, 71; prayed as a boy, 87; prayed often, 176

Nephites, 4, 9, 18

Oaks, Dallin H., 47–48

Obedience, 82, 124

Ocampo, Brother, story about, 53–56

"Oh, May My Soul Commune with Thee," 145–46

Operator, story about, 171–72

Opposition, 82

Packer, Boyd K., 157

Parents, 117, 119, 165–66

Patriarchal blessings, 178

Paul: on praying with thanksgiving, 28; on Spirit, 66, 97, 155; taught Joseph Smith, 67

Peace, 51, 80, 107–8, 137, 157

Perfection, 15, 71

Perspective: of God, 23, 24, 44, 137–38, 155; spiritual, 24–25

Peterson, H. Burke, 126

Pilot, story of, 112–13

Plan of Salvation, 134, 162

Pleading, 124–25

Ponder, 88

Prayer(s): intercessory, 1–5, 9, 31, 46, 52, 154; necessity of, 3, 7, 13; law of, 5; earnestness in, 5, 10–11, 25, 39, 150; to God the Father, 5–6, 7–8, 10; definition of, 5–6, 36–38; as commandment, 6, 8, 16, 37; blessings follow, 6–7; reasons for, 6–7, 15–20, 21, 133, 144–46; in name of Jesus Christ, 7, 52, 151; the Lord's, 8, 27–28, 118, 138; for family members, 9, 26, 52, 102, 119; for others, 9–10, 50, 77–78, 104; when and where to offer, 10, 16–18, 66, 76, 95, 156; personal, 10, 17, 68; public, 10, 17, 148–49; over food, 10, 123; how to offer, 10–11, 12, 27–28, 66; by power of Holy Ghost, 11; agency and, 11–12; formalities of, 12, 22, 25, 30, 47–48, 77, 86; and works, 12–14, 39–40, 50, 78, 147; as anchor, 13, 75; neglecting, 16–17, 35–36, 167–68; of children, 19–20, 118; for that which is right, 21; learning to offer, 23, 29–31, 53–56, 130; gaining experience in, 23–24, 31; learning from, 24, 29, 61, 155; content of, 24–25, 30–31, 42, 77; as work, 26, 37, 38–40, 46–47, 125, 177; for leaders, 26, 50, 77–78; of adoration,

27; for enemies, 27, 50; regular, 27, 151; that God's will be done, 28, 43, 102, 106–8, 127–28, 137–39, 163; about callings, 28, 79–80; unity in, 28, 58–59, 70, 103; as counseling with the Lord, 28–29; promptings during, 29, 48–49; blocks to, 29–30; for inappropriate things, 29–31, 42; about weaknesses, 30; and generalities, 30; conscience and, 30–31; for lost scriptures, 32–35; study on, and happiness, 35; as duty, 36; as natural, 36, 133; as blessing, 37; in morning, 37–38, 49, 151–52; as protection, 39; length of, 47, 49–50, 55, 59, 149–50; and repentance, 47, 94; meaningful, 48, 77, 148, 150; vocal, 49, 67, 149; strengthening, 49–52; brings peace, 51, 80, 107–8, 137, 157; asking questions during, 51–52; and feelings, 53, 56, 66–67; simplicity of, 60, 150; about what to pray for, 60–61; dedicatory, 60–61; temple as house of, 64; in desperate circumstances, 65, 83–84, 120, 147, 154, 164; spirit of, 66; silent, 66, 67, 76; when we don't feel like praying, 72, 76–77, 86, 106; never unworthy to offer, 73; and commandment to pray always, 73, 76, 95–96, 132, 147–48, 166–67, 175; reality of, 74; frequency of, 76; preparing for, 76–77, 86–92; about missionary work, 78–79; poem about, 80–81; invitation to, 83; and willingness to receive, 83; and going through motions, 84–85; formal, 96; teaching children to offer, 102, 117–25, 165–66; "telegraph," 103; for survival, 104; for healing, 107–8, 127, 142; for love, 110; four parts of, 118; sharing experiences with, 119, 123; as conversation, 130, 145; to understand ourselves, 145; barriers to, 146–47; respectful, 151; youth and, 152–53; kneeling during, 156; America founded on, 159–61; as calling home, 175–76. *See also* Answers; Family

prayer; Forgiveness; Listening; Thanksgiving
"Prayer Is the Soul's Sincere Desire," 13–14
Preparation: for second coming, 62; for prayer, 76, 86–92, 147; against fear, 113
Priorities, 146
Promptings, in prayer, 29, 48–49

Questions, 51–52

Rasmus, Carolyn J., 132
Relationships, 90
Repentance, 47, 94
Repetition: vain, 11, 30, 48, 68, 77, 100, 135; appropriate, 68
Resurrection, 4
Revelation, spirit of, 23–24
Richards, Willard, 65
Rock, John, 102
Romney, Marion G., 15, 24, 37

Sacrament, 60, 91, 94
Saints, praying to, 7
Salt Lake Temple, 69
Samuel, 26, 86, 178
Sanctification, 89, 108
Satan: and not praying, 36, 73, 106; resisting, 99; temptations of, 124; power of, 157
Saul, 26
Scriptures: story of lost, 32–35; reading, 90–91; answers come through, 101, 176–77; prompt us to pray, 106, 132–33; about trials, 128
Second coming, 61–62
Selflessness, 9–10, 23, 28
Sin: Christ suffered for, 2; and prayer, 13; and brother of Jared, 16–17; and Joseph Smith, 58, 70–71; forsaking, 90; losing desire for, 99. *See also* Forgiveness
Sincerity, 10–11
Sistine Chapel, 109
Smith, Alma, 141–42
Smith, Amanda, 141–42
Smith, Emma, 57–58, 64

Smith, George A., 69, 70

Smith, Joseph: addressed God the Father, 7, 18, 60; and translation, 11–12; and revelations on prayer, 16, 22, 35; on spirit of revelation, 23–24; prayed for forgiveness, 26–27; and James 1:5–6, 51, 161; letter from, to Emma, 57–58; prayer life of, 57–74; First Vision of, 58; weaknesses of, 58; length of prayers of, 59; prayed over johnnycake, 59; formal prayers of, 60; prayed about second coming, 61–62; prayed about suffering in Missouri, 62; and Martin Harris, 63; held family prayer, 63–64; prayed in desperate circumstances, 65; tarred and feathered, 65; prayed in gratitude, 65–66; and translation of Romans 8:26, 66–67, 97–98; became learned, 67; taught Hosanna Shout, 68; on Holy Ghost, 68–69; on loud prayers, 69–70; and vision of Savior, 72–73; as example, 73–74; testimony about, 78–79, 105; in Liberty Jail, 128; on simple prayers, 150

Smith, Joseph F., 22, 53

Snow, Eliza R., 63–64

Snow, Lorenzo, 69, 72

Spirit: teaches us to pray, 22, 35, 139, 149, 176; prayer brings, 37; responsiveness to, 61; assists in prayer, 66–67, 98, 155; outpouring of, in Kirtland, 72; answers come through, 78–79, 97; and scriptures, 91. See also Holy Ghost

Spirituality, 144

Stake presidents, choosing, 26

Stewardship, 28

Strivings, 66–67, 97, 155

Study, 88, 139–41

Stupor of thought, 88

Submission, 28, 107

Tanner, N. Eldon, 158

Telephone, story about, 170–71

Temple, 60–61, 64, 70

Temptation: necessity of, 26; praying to
avoid, 28, 76; is not sin, 99; escaping, 129; in youth, 152

Testimony, 8–9, 52, 54, 98

Thanksgiving: prayer of, 27, 37, 50–51, 95, 148, 164; after receiving answer, 46, 103–6; Joseph Smith and, 65–66; as commandment, 77; story of praying on, 121–23

Thurmond, Strom, 159–60, 161

Translation, 87–88

Trials, 126–31; praying to overcome, 26; of Joseph Smith, 65; come to everyone, 127; strength in, 129, 175

Truth, 24

Twelve Apostles: original, 3, 26, 28; latter-day, 72

United States of America, 159–60

Unity: in prayer, 28, 58–59, 103; as commandment, 70; in relationships, 92

Unworthiness, 73, 130

Voice, from heaven, 25

Wang, Julie, 93

Washington, George, 159

Water, 51, 85

Weaknesses, 30, 58, 90

Welfare, 79–80

Woodruff, Wilford, 64

Words: vain, 84–85, 100; finding, 98, 138; and thoughts, 150, worshiping only with, 162

Work, prayer as, 26, 37, 38–40, 46–47, 125, 177. See also Study

Works: must match prayers, 12–14, 147; good, 39–40, 50, 77

World War II: story of sailor in, 114–15; story of family prayer during, 121–22

Worthiness, 73, 149

Young, Brigham, 36, 38

Young Women logo, 140–41

Zenos, 150–51

Zion, 116